THE DISAPPEARANCE

CARMEN BARTON

Paperback: 978-1-967820-96-2
Hardcover: 978-1-968667-45-0
eBook: 978-1-967820-97-9
Library of Congress Control Number: 2025916458

This is a work of fiction.

Ordering Information:

Prime Seven Media
518 Landmann St.
Tomah City, WI 54660

Printed in the United States of America

Blessed are the pure in heart, for they will see God.

Matthew 5:8

"Heaven always vindicates the heart that loves purely."

Table of Contents

Introduction

*I*n response to your call today and your request to write down what's happening, here's my story. I'll start at the beginning so you can understand everything properly. Everything I say is based on the truth unless explicitly stated. I'm not 100% certain about some things, but I have a strong suspicion, in which case I'll clearly indicate this in the text.

It began in April, Uden.

The parents I grew up with were not my biological parents.

My biological father was most likely Jan van Herpen, a half-brother of my foster father. Jan was a priest and missionary in Brazil for a long time. He had a girlfriend there, her name was Carmen.

Jan lived in the castle in Gemert for a long time, until he left the order and married—not Carmen, which was impossible, mainly because of the distance. When he resigned his priesthood, he was forced to return to the Netherlands, making it impossible for the two lovebirds to be together any longer. People were looking for other solutions; having illegitimate children was considered a disgrace at the time, especially in those circles, especially for a priest.

It was not uncommon for clergy within the Catholic Church to maintain a partner and a substantial amount of money. This was also the case with Jan. His work in Brazil was more than exceptionally impressive, although after his departure from the Netherlands, he was ignored and miscommunicated everywhere. How painful that must have been for him. Brazilians came to him with everything during that time, from childbirth and all sorts of medical matters to advice on just about anything. Carmen often helped him with this; she was a nurse. The two were madly in love. My foster mother often received letters from Jan about it. During that time, he and Carmen would take a boat trip across the Amazon River for three days every month to visit a leper camp. This was right through the Amazon region, which was extremely dangerous. Just think of the crocodiles in the river, not to mention the rest of the rainforest. The destination was even scarier, although I do think he was vaccinated, at least immune, but still.

Leaving the order was difficult for him, and returning to the Netherlands was equally difficult, only to rebuild a normal life. He wasn't allowed to grow old. He died just a few years after I'd finished studying in Maastricht, at the university founded by a pediatrician from Gemert who was also its rector for a time. Shortly before Jan died, I visited him in the imposing villa where he was living at the time.

Jan's executor, his much younger half-brother Theo, clearly enjoyed a very comfortable life. There was hardly any division, and I certainly never saw a cent. That had been Jan's intention, though. The notary in Heesch knew what to do with it.

Apparently, I have a brother who received some money from Theo, a relatively small sum. Theo's children drove around in a

Jaguar, and they were crazy and didn't know what to do with all the money, so they bought the craziest things, like a camper van that was always parked in front of the house because no one ever took it on a trip. Helping others never even crossed their minds, let alone sharing fairly. While I didn't even have money for textbooks because of poverty, I always had to study in the study hall, which was a lot of fun, of course, but studying didn't always work out.

I was treated poorly at home, although my foster mother did her best. For a while, it seemed like my life would end in a clinic where, due to years of abuse, I had to be admitted to my home on weekends.

It didn't stop there. After I graduated, they forced me to take Richard in. I loved him very much, but his past had been very troublesome, and his ex-in-laws kept harassing us for money; the children, in particular, were used to spy on us. It got to the point that his daughter-in-law managed to seduce him, making him completely ill, even literally.

At one point, I had to go to the hospital at night with a brain injury.

Richard had suffered a psychotic episode after his children had had far too many children in a short period of time; it was one pregnancy after another. It was especially the contact with Richard's ex-in-laws and the desire of both grandparents, Richard and Hedy, to form a large family together that completely blew Richard's mind. The fact that I had pulled Richard out of a very deep pit and given him a whole new life didn't matter to them at the time, nor did the deep love that also existed between him and me. He had always been very easily influenced, especially when it came to his children. I just had to be removed, so his ex could take my place—it not only seemed that way, but it was.

I took a taxi to the hospital in Helmond.

The next morning, very early, after I had spent hours outside in the cold because they couldn't help me in the emergency room, Richard came to pick me up, mind you. I also saw his daughter-in-law at that unusual hour, six in the morning, passing the intersection near the hospital where I was waiting for Richard, just before he arrived. God ultimately punished them both. Now, however, my foster mother has also passed away. She absolutely did not deserve to be punished, although it was a kind of redemption. She, too, was severely abused by my half-sister and my foster father. The division of the inheritance is again anything but fair, a Van Herpen affair.

Whenever I visited my foster mother, I was invariably kicked out by my foster father. I was not allowed to provide care for her. She went through hell, a hardship and great sorrow for me. My first impression was that alerting the authorities had little or no effect. Because of the incorrect diagnosis they had also given me, I could not file a report. They invariably sent the same woman from the outreach service, who initially also preferred to keep me under wraps, meaning silenced.

Because of my political party membership, my foster family had an additional reason to want to kill me as well.

My foster father recently said it literally: "Now you're at the top of my list, now it's your turn!" He never did much good for me, if this was still well-intentioned after all these years I'd eat my hat, I'm not often wrong.

And I've never done anything wrong. What's making it difficult for me is the settlement of yet another inheritance dispute that isn't being handled fairly. I had to sell my car, a beautiful Volvo, because it was vandalized. There have been burglaries, robberies, and vandalism at my home. The grave of my husband, Richard, was desecrated several times, all of which was deeply painful. That's why I wrote this book. Writing helps, I recommend it to everyone; paper is patient.

Part I
Green

*T*his book begins with a prayer:

"Only today can I begin to improve my life. Procrastination is pointless and only makes things worse. I only have to do the good, and the bad will sooner be forgotten. I have no other choice. Because if I don't do this, one day I will be punished, by people or by God, one of the two. There's no escape, one way or another. With a toothache, if I eat too much candy; with being overweight, if I eat too much; with lung cancer, if I smoke; and so on. Yes, or rather, I'd rather not, because it's all lust and unhealthy, devilish, actually. It applies to many things in life. Not just when you're talking about food or stimulants; there are many forms of behavior that certainly don't contribute to your well-being or happiness. One day it will be punished. Bad behavior has consequences, sometimes serious. Sooner or later you'll be called to account, and that's also the moment when God will judge.

I have no choice but to do what is good. After all, God sees everything. He can tear the hairs out of your hair. You can count your head and God always has the final say. People can only think they can control everything. It's an illusion; things always turn out differently, sometimes a little, sometimes a lot. There are always circumstances you hadn't anticipated.

Just as an epidemiologist maps out the possible causes of certain diseases, it remains a matter of conjecture to a certain extent. We can try to understand everything, but humans will never fully succeed.

God is great, the universe is great, and not even the only one. We cannot fathom God. We will never understand where it all began and where it ends. Of course, we have a calendar that began with Christ, but that's a completely different story, which was about God's people. As everyone knows, there were multiple groups of peoples on earth, a kind of family, usually separate from each other. One group of people was usually not related to the other; they were large groups of people, who lived together, usually not in close proximity to other groups. They moved around, as God's people were, convinced they were right and guided by God. He took them by the hand daily. Although they didn't always listen very well. After the birth of Christ, people became increasingly open to people from other ethnic groups, and slowly the Word of God spread throughout the world.

There was a time in history when people became arrogant and wanted to demonstrate their power by building a tower that reached the heavens, a long time ago, thousands of years ago. God wanted to prevent people from building the tower; he saw that they had become arrogant and thought they no longer needed Him. To prevent humanity from becoming even more powerful, God threw a wrench in the works by causing confusion. This resulted in people, and especially the builders of the tower, being unable to do their work properly because they didn't understand each other well. The construction of the Tower of Babel was therefore abandoned, and people began to disperse to the four corners of the earth. The confusion resulted in a confusion of tongues, and people began speaking all sorts of different languages, while humanity initially spoke much more of a single language.

The wisdom passed down through the generations over the centuries is recorded in the Bible; no single book against it, it is a very great, important source of knowledge, about life and death, but above all about God.

If I do good things, they will come my way. It's the only way; there really is no other way. Anyone who wants to know God must read the Bible; there's no escaping it. The Bible is fundamentally different from any other book and is full of divine wisdom, which won't surprise you. Divine wisdom, however, is quite different from human wisdom. To clarify the distinction, you could say that divine wisdom has a lot to do with intuition, the sixth sense, while human wisdom is not much more than knowing and understanding a lot of facts. Gaining knowledge about a particular subject can be relevant in various professions, but divine wisdom is much more relevant to life in a broader sense, how to find happiness, and what you should and shouldn't do. It's all described in the Bible, especially the Old Testament book of Proverbs, which is brimming with wisdom, very instructive, and applicable at all times. Because anyone who thinks the Bible is an outdated book is completely mistaken; no book is relevant to the times we live in anymore. God forgives—in the name of Christ—bad things people may have done, especially if they strive to do good. All bad fades into the background when you show good will and express remorse, thus creating new opportunities for yourself. Through the birth of Christ, people are forgiven of sins. One can ask forgiveness in the name of Christ, and your name will then be cleared, although it is certainly important to demonstrate that things can be done differently. It is important that one improves one's attitude in certain cases, or at least works on it, otherwise, people might continue to sin. That is not the intention; those times are long gone. God is currently judging; repenting now is practically too late.

Christ was a good example. God sent His only Son to earth to grant people forgiveness; no other religion works that way. You could also say God sacrificed His Son, because Christ had to suffer terribly to help humanity; for that reason alone, He will never be forgotten. Anyone can become a Christian. You can ask God for forgiveness and pray in Christ's name, and then your name will be cleared. God forgives you, so you must also forgive others and yourself.

It's the only way to make something of your life, and you will be rewarded. Heaven will open, wealth and happiness will be yours, lack will be no more, and God will reward you eternally.

You can't change the past; leaving it behind is better. Whatever you do, the past will never return.

Be grateful for everything you have, try to learn from what you experience, look at what you do have, let go of what you've lost. Sometimes it can be helpful to reflect on the past to process it.

Dwelling on hatred and sorrow is pointless. God will judge, something we as humans can hardly, if at all, do. God's ways are inscrutable. We can try to understand them, but we will never fully succeed. One day we will all be together again, somewhere in the universe, in some universe, where it is much more beautiful and wonderful than here on Earth."

The Vegetable Garden

Over the past few years, I've taken dozens of wonderful walks with Benny. I knew him from a hospitalization thirty-five years ago, when I had to be admitted to my home due to abuse. I ran into him regularly when I visited Richard many years later, decades actually. Benny became my rock and support during that time. The park near the institution is beautiful and lent itself to inspiring walks, which I thoroughly enjoyed. We went on many walks together, especially after Richard passed away.

One day, Emmy was there too. She contacted me. In retrospect, she was a rather problematic person. Begging was no problem for her, and it felt manipulative when she wanted to meet up and, at the end of each conversation, ordered me to bring all sorts of things. While it's good for someone to express their needs, it can also be done differently. When you pray, be clear; otherwise, God doesn't know how to help. You can compare it to that. In the Dutch welfare state, although in decline, I find it much more comforting to discuss this in a normal way, with less manipulation. She had been through a lot in her life, which explained her behavior, and none of it had been her fault, at least not in her opinion. This is true, although everyone has a task in life to let go of the past, and everyone gets their share, difficulties often become the most important learning opportunities.

She was taking fentanyl, a highly dangerous and extremely addictive substance that is now added to many drugs to make them even more addictive. It's almost a thousand times stronger than heroin, and people are dying in the streets in some American cities. Philadelphia is a case in point; in the Kensington neighborhood, it's commonplace—inhumane situations, really. Fentanyl is also available by prescription, which makes its use at least somewhat safer, although it remains a life-threatening drug. It's prescribed for pain management, for example, and is also considerably stronger than morphine. Stopping it is practically impossible, at least not without help.

It was introduced in the early 1960s by the Belgian pharmaceutical company Jansen and later acquired by another pharmaceutical company. Initially, the drug was primarily used in the animal industry due to its incredibly potent effects—a heavy-handed drug. Later, it found its way into healthcare and now also into the drug world, where it has truly fallen into the wrong hands, being abused by dealers.

Not every invention is an improvement, as is once again evident.

The same company recently paid eight billion dollars in damages to someone in Canada because of the drug Risperdal, which they also wrongly forced me to take for a long time. It has a terrible number of side effects, hence the compensation.

Not that I received anything like that; legally, it's often a long process to achieve something like that, or rather, I didn't see a cent of it.

Perhaps I should have. This might be a relative of mine, a cousin posing as a brother and perhaps biologically more than just a cousin, I don't know. In any case, he does live in Canada.

It is a fact that our family is complicated, and the fact that he called me at that time to say that 'Uncle Jan' also had a son is also a striking fact.

And furthermore, they had a great deal of information about my life, possibly through the book my foster family had written about me, based on stolen medical records and diaries stolen from my foster father (!), a book full of lies and deceit, very serious libel. It might have been written for that reason, to extract compensation. My foster mother was completely kept out of this; she knew nothing, although after so many events, a lightbulb finally came to her mind.

My foster sister has a forest, which tells you something; you don't just acquire a forest just like that. Or a wine chateau, an estate in South Africa, entire countries and half continents, God knows. You don't find out, they say nothing. If there's any omerta, it's within this family, which is otherwise a fragmented whole.

It makes them suspicious, suspicious because I haven't seen a cent of that money, and why should he get it? Our paths haven't crossed very often. At that time, he sold his house to find another one. He vacationed in Florida with his entire family, but he preferred not to have any contact with me, except occasionally when something needed to be discussed.

Now I've been completely miscommunicated by my family, in a terribly inhumane way, the details of which I'll leave aside here. It's bad enough as it is, I don't need to reopen that wound. Perhaps that's my good fortune now, that a burden has been lifted from my shoulders. They only cause trouble, and they know very little decency. Fortunately, this doesn't apply to all my family members; there are still some who do mean well.

The fact is it's the same story every time. It seems to be all about taking money from each other. Truly awful, and some of them can act just as pathetic as many asylum seekers, some of whom are nothing more than fortune seekers. They're unparalleled actors who can evoke pity. In Hollywood, they would be fully realized, although no one wants such egotists. And that's putting it mildly.

Fentanyl withdrawal is only possible under supervision, and even then it's incredibly difficult. It destroys a lot of things in your body due to the incredibly powerful anesthetic.

Pain is a signal, indicating that a limit has been reached. Due to the use or administration of painkillers, signals in your body disappear, you no longer feel the overload, sometimes with very serious consequences; you cross boundaries. This can cause serious tissue damage, meaning you need increasingly more of a particular substance to feel even remotely good. With powerful substances like fentanyl, at a certain point, there's a point where you can't hold on anymore; the impact is so great that it's unmanageable. In many cases, withdrawal is virtually impossible, at least without supervision.

Daily doses are also much more frequent than with heroin, for example; one has to take a certain dose much more often to feel even remotely good. I certainly don't mean to condone heroin; it's all harmful, and moreover, heroin now also contains fentanyl. Things are going in the wrong direction in that regard. Even one wrong dose can be fatal. Staying away from it is wisest, and at least quitting if necessary.

The main problem is that it's added to so many drugs, precisely because it's so addictive. You could argue that this makes illegal drug producers and dealers even more criminal, because this is, of course, done deliberately to make even more money. The fact that this drug is used in medicine is also a problem. Addicts always look for ways to obtain certain substances. In Emmy's case, this could unintentionally make her a target for criminals. It's not inconceivable that a criminal, for example, would contact her to obtain the drug. Addicts sometimes do the strangest things to obtain their daily fix. In an emergency, calling someone who might be in possession of this drug doesn't seem like a startling prospect, but it is something to consider.

Yes, and I'm investigating the Tanja Groen case. And Emmy, believe it or not, is possibly a distant relative of mine in some way; she was born in Uden.

There's a certain synchrony in my life with that of Tanja Groen, a young student who disappeared during a student orientation and was never heard from again, but certainly also with that of Emmy, for some obscure reason. There's a whole network of people, controlled by family, who want to stop my publications. Contact between Emmy and, yes, family, wouldn't surprise me; I've found evidence of that. She revealed all sorts of things, especially during our last conversation: from the emotional age of someone close to me to the number of rusks I eat per day; the kind of cheese I sometimes buy, cream cheese for making cheesecake; that I pay close attention to the expiration date; sometimes

I use a digital flashlight if I can't see something clearly. The craziest things she couldn't possibly know—it's almost inevitable that family members have also contacted her behind my back. It doesn't surprise me, because I've seen it happen many times before: they contact my friends behind my back. They think it's perfectly normal, but they don't have good intentions, not just to clean up their own mess.

And even then, these are largely things they normally wouldn't know; there's much more to this. To put it mildly, the fact that my foster father asked my deceased husband, Richard, to take my life was the absolute lowest point, of course without my knowledge.

Richard told me this when he was dying and gave a very long confession. I wasn't even surprised anymore, although it is certainly too awful to put into words.

They always know how to corner you with their kind words and excessive kindness, trying to figure out what you're doing or whatever, to extract information. And of course, exceptions prove the rule, and there are certainly a lot of good, honest people in my family, sometimes unaware of any wrongdoing. But even then, you have to be careful, especially when it comes to sharing certain information.

Towards the end of his life, I discovered that Richard had known my family much longer than I had known him.

My suspicion arose when I discovered that the name Van Tongeren appeared in my deceased husband's ex-in-laws, who had been married before.

My foster mother's father's girlfriend was also named Van Tongeren. He moved in with her sometime after my grandmother, my foster mother's mother, passed away.

It wasn't a good match; they absolutely couldn't get along. For a long time, Grandpa still rented a house as a possible escape. When they finally moved in together, things went terribly wrong; he died under suspicious circumstances. That all happened long before I met Richard, about ten years earlier.

I met Richard in the mid-nineties through a friend.

Grandpa died in the late eighties.

Tanja Groen disappeared in the early nineties; I didn't know Richard then either.

My family had known Richard for much longer, of course. There's a lot to suggest it, and Richard told me about it too.

Shortly after I moved in with Richard, we went to Brussels for a weekend. Richard's ex-wife's new partner also worked there. We stayed overnight at the Holiday Inn Hotel, not far from the airport.

I didn't have a good feeling about that weekend; strange things happened. For example, several men suddenly showed up in the hotel room. I constantly felt like I had to get myself out of all sorts of dire situations.

Many years later, Richard told me that my foster father had asked him to kill me. That explains a lot. Probably a long time before I met him.

Richard was a poor artist at that time. Ultimately, he was a good-hearted person, but many people had taken advantage of him; he was easily influenced, and that was perhaps his biggest problem. He always believed everyone. If someone said to him, "What a beautiful painting you've made!" he already assumed they wanted to buy it. It was also a way of thinking positively, so you could look at it differently, visualize it, and it often worked. Even if you initially thought, Richard, that man or woman only says it's a beautiful work.

He had tried (often), he said, to kill me, but he couldn't.

This can be explained in two ways: he couldn't because I sensed it and reacted to it, for example, by being very cautious and keeping my distance; you could also say he couldn't because of pangs of conscience; it touched his heart, and he had genuinely grown to love me. This was mutual, although I was more or less forced to live with him at the time, which was completely unlawful. Several nurses were behind it. Van den E was one of them, and it wasn't right. It should never have happened that I was forced into this. The apartment I rented was private, not owned by the institution. He had been head nurse at De Wijst, a social housing facility where Richard lived for a long time. Later, he became a practice supervisor at the general practice I was affiliated with, and as such, I had to deal with him again later. It was the moment that Richard's severe psychosis was completely ignored, with all its dire consequences. "Moment" isn't really the right word; this dire situation persisted for a full eight years, until Richard finally died. The general practitioner only came to personally inquire after seven years, and Van der E was even less interested; he had made up his own story.

They had no right to force me to take someone in, but I had no choice at that moment. All that time, I had mixed feelings about it. On the one hand, I grew to love Richard, but on the other, I always felt uneasy, a sense that something wasn't right, that I couldn't fully trust him. In retrospect, you could say my hunch was right.

In those circles, that part of healthcare, they actually want to take away your intuition, although that's become commonplace these days. Thinking for yourself is barely allowed, and believing in God is even more so; otherwise, you're considered crazy. You're almost literally stripped bare, and they won't leave a splinter of you if you're not careful. But they also do good work. Precisely because of those razor-sharp analyses, they're able to pinpoint the sore spot and give your life a new lease on life. And not only that, but sometimes a completely different direction, including a different name—that happens too. They had formed a whole network called The Circle, one of whom worked at the institution in question, and they caused me a lot of misery. When, a long time ago, during my student days, I was completely wrongly abused at home on weekends—for no apparent reason and certainly not my fault—that I had to be admitted to hospital, I was misdiagnosed due to lies and deceit from my foster family and corruption within the institution, and it changed my life forever.

Fresh out of university, with a medical degree under my belt, after years of hard work, I ended up in a closed ward with mostly criminals; I didn't belong there. Fortunately, they managed to save my life there, because it was hanging by a thread, so severely had I been abused. Fortunately, I was quickly transferred to an open ward.

But it didn't stop there. These unpleasant situations, which were solely about possessions and money (a literal inheritance issue) to which they had no right and which they took from me, continue to this day, almost forty years later. I can barely remember anything else, and it seems to be getting worse and worse, it seems, it's only getting worse, hence this book. It didn't stop there; recently, I was the victim of vandalism, burglary, and even desecration of my husband's grave. His grave has been vandalized several times.

Over possessions and money, out of jealousy, by people who misunderstood much of life, or at least don't know how things are supposed to be, and with whom I have now permanently broken off contact.

These kinds of institutions, psychiatric hospitals, often house people who have been rejected by family, victims of domestic violence, in fact, for all sorts of reasons, one of which is an inheritance issue. Family members are often easily vindicated; they are in the majority and the patient or client can barely defend themselves, simply because of the often forced medication, and they don't always receive the same level of protection. The clinic is happy with yet another patient who brings in money, a life-threatening situation, and in some cases, which I also consider mine, summary execution without any form of trial.

The Circle is part of a much larger network, with ties to the World Economic Forum (WEF). The fact is that they were involved in criminal offenses, one of which was child abuse. To induce people to take care of all sorts of things, they offered them rewards in return.

The prospect that all of this has very little to do with honest, fair, and especially transparent conduct speaks for itself. Because if anyone wanted to leave or develop a different opinion, they were pulled over and reminded of the moments they had so delightfully enjoyed all the privileges, often things that were better kept secret; they were happy to avoid them.

What is so striking, partly because of this, is the culture of cover-up in all kinds of crime and police cases in the Netherlands. It sometimes seemed as if almost everyone in the justice system had been infected with it, and public funds were being abused on a massive scale. Civil servants were bribed, and the question wasn't whether someone had done something, if it involved a criminal offense, but rather how they could quietly make that file disappear without anyone batting an eye.

A retired high-ranking official in the Dutch justice system was often identified as a suspect in the media in the past, especially in all kinds of cases related to pedophilia, particularly the abuse of young boys. He was indeed also spotted at times in the Anne Frank Park in Eindhoven, where young boys offered sexual services.

This is in addition to the WEF's Agenda Twenty-Thirty, which aims for a "better world," which many people question, not only because of the speed with which the program was pushed through on a global scale, using every means necessary.

It is also due to the simultaneous non-commitment of this ragtag grouping of the very wealthy and powerful, primarily representatives of the pharmaceutical industry. It seems more like a global coup than a fair, equitable representation of participating countries. The organization isn't based on participating countries at all; no, that's what the World Cup and the Olympic Games are for; this is a completely different ballgame. The WEF participants largely consist of shareholders in the pharmaceutical industry. The WEF has very strong ties with the WHO, which, while far more legitimately international in character, has fallen out of the blue, while simultaneously bowing down to the WEF, which was completely unknown twenty years ago and emerged from the Bilderberg Group, and which still exists as such.

The WEF also has very strong ties with the EU, which is not surprising given that current European President Von der Leyen is married to someone who holds a prominent position in the pharmaceutical industry—that's quite a double entendre.

NATO has also partially joined this collective, although US President Donald Trump at one point made moves to withdraw entirely. Especially within the WEF and the EU, they pretend to represent the majority with a good cause in mind, but the reality is one of a dictatorial regime, a totalitarian one in which no one has any say except the leaders of this group of eccentrics themselves. You could easily argue that we're back to slavery, and perhaps that's also why they're currently pumping Europe full of Africans, mainly to remind us of that and retroactively instill guilt again and again about something that happened centuries ago and whose status was already questionable back then. I'm not saying that slaves were treated so well, but that many were happy to flee their homeland, hoping for a better future, and in some cases, they found it.

The Thousand-Year Reich is still being implemented, while everyone looks the other way. You're no longer allowed to have an opinion; you run a high risk of being eliminated, as they so politely put it, either killed, or in a hospital in a "decent" manner—which sometimes happened—or by outright criminals in a less "decent" but often equally criminal way. Once part of this intimidating circle, there's virtually no way back. People are completely cornered, and anyone who spills the beans risks being mercilessly punished.

The strange plans of this powerful organization include the idea that no one will own any property, except themselves, of course. In their case, the money only goes one way; the rest belongs to the community—at least, that's the plan. Still, something God would never sign up for, because of the injustice of it. Let them chatter and feel safe in their self-created dream world—where no one owns anything but themselves—which has little to do with reality, even though they're well on their way to realizing their dreams because everyone falls for it. People, especially older people, are simply not used to governments being almost untrustworthy anymore and everything on television becoming completely unbelievable after several layers of censorship.

Meanwhile, another entire country lies in ruins, which was completely unnecessary; diplomatic solutions were easily devised.

If you boil this down to the micro level, often a way to gain more insight, it's strange that, for example, in the case of a vegetable garden, anyone could just pick your harvest.

This means that bad behavior is rewarded—in this case, stealing someone's carefully grown vegetables, fruit, or herbs—while good behavior is punished—the act of growing them, sometimes with blood, sweat, and tears. Where are we going to stay in this world like this? God would never approve of that, and God doesn't approve of it, I can assure you. God is a just God. And God has the final say; there's simply no arguing about that. People with these kinds of ideas will one day fall into the same pit they dug for someone else; there's no escaping it. In the case of a vegetable garden, almost literally.

Emmy called me yesterday to join her for a walk, although she did say she wasn't feeling well. I realized this when I arrived; her behavior was downright abnormal, extremely suspicious, and extremely strange.

During the walk, she contradicted me on everything, and I barely had a chance to say anything. Moreover, it was a miracle she even came along. It wouldn't have been the first time she'd left me out in the cold after a half-hour bike ride.

I don't have a car anymore; they destroyed it out of jealousy, and I didn't just have a car, one you only buy once in a lifetime.

If you don't grant anyone else anything, you'll never have anything yourself; that's where it all begins. Make someone else rich first and the money comes much more easily.

Moreover, it's better to let go of money and consider the quality of what you're doing; that's much more important. Gaining knowledge, then the money will come naturally.

Emmy's behavior reminded me of someone—sick, psychopathic, actually—the behavior of a narcissist.

Every time I tried to say anything again after fifteen minutes of listening, I was immediately and resoundingly silenced, for example, because she kept talking over me.

This is painful for me because I've experienced this many times with someone and felt like I was never able to express my opinion in a normal, calm, and well-argued way. I was always interrupted by that person, which is very sick and very rude. That's certainly not how I learned it.

We used to live on an island for a long time at home, everyone going their own way. As children, we attended different schools, pursued different courses, and were members of different clubs.

At dinnertime, our paths would cross, and things would usually get heated quickly, though not literally. My mother was a very good cook; it was something she learned from childhood in the butcher shop.

Grandpa also had a slaughterhouse. He regularly went to the cattle market to buy cows himself. When we went there on Sundays when we were very young, we were allowed to play there. It was always freezing cold, not only because of the sight of all those halved cow carcasses hanging from immense meat hooks, but also because of the temperature, which prevented the meat from spoiling. Once the meat was boned, the waste went to a dump behind the slaughterhouse, which you'd rather stay away from; the smell was unbearable. We didn't have much time to explore there either; we usually also visited the other grandfather. He owned a stationery store and sold pens, paper, and other stationery, as well as toys. Yes, that was certainly quite interesting at that age. But with thirty other nieces and nephews, you couldn't expect to get anything; we were allowed to browse, and that's usually all it was. When my mother got into the art business, I took over the kitchen job at a young age.

Richard was head chef in the NATO officers' kitchen for many years. I learned all the tricks of the trade from him, although my mother was very good at preparing meat, even beef tongue. I can still see Richard shivering at that; he loved tongue, but not quite in the literal sense of the word...

We had ended up in an immense vegetable garden. Although not much grew there in the winter, especially with all that snow, the outlines of many vegetables and herbs were still clearly visible. Emmy asked me almost ten times if I wanted to take something home, and I felt like I had to bend over backwards to refuse her "generous" offer; some people suddenly become very generous when they can share other people's things. Although picking one of those plants would certainly have been another way for her, with what seemed like a pure heart, to pull a knife from her coat pocket, as had happened once before when I, too, had been there after I'd agreed to it after asking it to me many times, only to be caught by the farmer a while later. I really felt too old for that by now and thought it wasn't worth the effort, literally in this case.

The kale, though covered in a layer of snow, was still standing relatively upright. She kept asking. Taking someone else's vegetables isn't allowed. That one time she managed to persuade me, she told me she'd gotten permission to take a few things.

It was strange that this time, after asking so many times, she finally emphatically stated that she'd gotten permission herself and that it definitely didn't apply to me. Bam, another slap in the face. I hadn't even planned on it; emphasizing it this way was completely unnecessary. She clearly wanted to set a trap. We'd been wandering around in that garden for almost an hour, even though I hadn't noticed anything at the time. Her claims were very ambiguous, as if she wanted to warn me at the same time, and perhaps she did, although she certainly wasn't in a good mood. The kindness was abundantly clear from the moment I stopped bringing her tobacco. It seemed more like someone else had taken over my role in that regard; she certainly couldn't live without it, as was her precarious financial situation.

People in similar situations have had it especially tough since the enormous excise tax increases on tobacco products in the Netherlands. It's the combination of pills and tobacco that makes it so difficult for them to quit smoking, while at the same time, it has become unaffordable for this group. Some people are so severely addicted that they would literally kill for a pack of cigarettes. Yes, and there she was again, a cigarette in her mouth, smoking non-stop. I often wondered how she could afford it all.

Suddenly, there she was, standing in front of me with a razor-sharp Stanley knife. Well, sharp! It was fortunate she couldn't get the blade out; perhaps it had gotten stuck in the cold; it had snowed that day. It looked quite new and must have been sharp, I assume. How she got the knife is a mystery, although it's certainly not common for people in such situations to possess such knives, though it could be worse.

When Benny let me in to show him his apartment once, I was shocked by the mess. His room looked like a cross between an ironworks (gas bottle included) and a thrift store, with a pristine white single bed in the middle. Not exactly safe to have a gas bottle next to your bed at night; he was busy with it when I visited him again. Going to sleep in that same air again at night is, of course, far from ideal. And what about the neighbors? The walls there were almost made of cardboard—not a place to feel very comfortable. His garden wasn't much better and gave the same impression. A nurse I once confronted about it said he knew nothing when I asked how things had gotten so out of hand, saying he was a substitute. They'd clearly abandoned Benny to his fate that much was clear. Although he once studied philosophy, things had indeed gotten completely out of hand, also a kind of inheritance issue. His brothers and sister had all ended up well in high positions and barely paid any attention to him.

Just try to come to terms with that as a patient in such an institution: you have no say, getting out is impossible, a hopeless situation. Benny's neighbor must have felt the same way when she voluntarily took her own life. They're happy to give you a push, even though they'll vehemently deny it. And that's not necessary; things can be different, especially if people start accepting that different is also normal, that people have the right to an opinion and a decent life. The pills they're given, though sometimes necessary in certain cases, partially halt brain function, or at best, slow it down.

She had a huge wad of toilet paper in her pocket and two coats on. The first was probably meant to stop the bleeding and the second to cover a potential corpse. I could tell something was wrong, and perhaps a lot of things were wrong.

All in all, it seemed like an almost laughable attempt on her part to commit an attack, although at the same time, it might have been seriously intended and anything but funny. Unconsciously, I had been keeping a considerable physical distance the whole time.

However, she bent over backwards to literally seek closeness, coming up with strange reasons for doing so. Her behavior was truly odd. She constantly asked me to read all sorts of texts on her phone, which she then looked up again, even forcing me to read certain passages multiple times. She was also on the phone when I wasn't paying attention. Hidden behind a bush, she was talking to someone, whispering, really. When she saw me notice, she quickly hung up. You could have said something about the whole incident: a person without training or qualifications, without understanding, or refused to use it.

There had been some kind of introduction beforehand, some story about a police officer who had agreed with her in a certain situation after she'd called the police over the weekend. She also said she often went to the vet and didn't mind consulting one on the weekend. A kind of mutation of Munchausen Syndrome by Proxy: one seeks attention for the pet, but actually indirectly for oneself. And constantly consulting the vet, even when one knows one can't afford it.

It was a torrent of disjointed stories in which self-pity seemed to be a recurring theme, and I get it; her childhood wasn't easy, nor was her entire life. She never had to work, but otherwise doesn't do much; all she does is complain.

The gist of her story, however, was also, when I look back on it all, that no one would ever support me if something happened because I'd taken a psychiatric patient for a walk. Everyone, including the police, would have told me I should have known better; they're looking for ways out. Yes, and as an evangelist, you do such things, you try to help even the most impossible people, although certainly not everything was wrong; she provided me with valuable information. It doesn't matter anyway, because of that admission thirty years ago and the wrong diagnosis they gave me, I can't file a report anyway, completely wrongly, not even now that the diagnosis has been revised because people have become aware that there wasn't much of it right.

She realized she couldn't touch me, literally, and suddenly acted like she'd found the knife out of nowhere. I walked away from a fence with her, and not even two seconds later, she had the knife in her hands. I didn't see her pick it up anywhere, nor did she express genuine surprise at finding it. That simply couldn't be. She said she'd seen it lying around somewhere, but there was probably little truth in what she was saying; it was completely unbelievable. And then there was that enormous wad of toilet paper in her jacket pocket. Could that really have been her plan, to stop the bleeding? I think so. She was constantly on her phone and tried all sorts of ways, which became very annoying, to get physically close to me, including touching. The way my foster family, all my life, has been trying to contact people I'm in contact with behind my back is horrific, even with my neighbors. They usually avoid talking to me directly. She probably intended to run and stab the knife into my back, but it literally stuck, or at least it faltered before she could do anything with it, which was my luck. When I turned around, she was standing there with a knife in her hands that wasn't working properly. She probably quickly made up the excuse that she'd found it.

She then wanted to put it away somewhere, supposedly so the workers would find it, but she mainly put it away so no one would see it and she could safely retrieve it herself. The walk ended with a verbal altercation from her. Dismayed, I ran off to grab my bike and rush home. I felt distraught and wondered what I'd done wrong, but nothing. I'd selflessly tried to help her recently, which had cost me a lot of money, twenty-three euros for a pack of rolling tobacco, and that wasn't all. From now on, I'll stay away from bad people and have become more selective about whom I let into my life. The Bible also says so. It also states that you should especially watch out for people who are overly friendly; they often have a hidden agenda and a lot to hide. The same goes for people who get angry quickly. It seems the opposite, but it often starts with excessive friendliness that can quickly turn sour. If you utter a single wrong word, you could almost literally be decapitated. Such people exist, and it's best to stay away from them. Being so overly friendly is also very insincere and, of course, not sustainable for long. Richard sometimes had a bit of a habit of it around my birthday. Forgive me, I owe him a lot of good things, but I'll give this as an example. On my birthday, he behaved perfectly, like the ideal husband—so perfectly that it became uncomfortable. However, the hangover usually came a day later, after the birthday was over. I'd just gotten used to his friendliness and then had to settle for his normal attitude, with much less attention. At some point, we stopped celebrating birthdays. We were always together; he was the artist. If I suddenly, even for a day, was put on a pedestal, he didn't quite know what to do. Although external factors played a major role in the decision to stop celebrating birthdays. When I turned fifty, he gave me a car, which I'll never forget, and I enjoyed it for a long time. It was a bit of a shock at first when we discovered that shortly after buying it, we'd spent as much on repairs as on the purchase price. Don't worry, it was well-intentioned, and I ultimately enjoyed it for five years without any significant problems until he finally gave it up. We even drove it to Spain once, our last holiday together.

It wasn't the first time I'd gotten into trouble in a vegetable garden somewhere.

The Allotment Gardens

My husband had just passed away, and I was devastated. By chance, a neighbor mentioned the new allotment garden complex in the village, which still had a few plots available. It sounded like a good idea, if only for a distraction, but also because of the coronavirus crisis at the time, I thought it would be a good idea to start growing my own vegetables.

I enthusiastically got started and chose the largest plot available, next to my neighbor's, who obviously also had a plot of land there; otherwise, I certainly wouldn't have gotten this far. It was my first real vegetable garden, and I still had a lot to learn. This was grist to the neighbor's mill, who promised to show me the ropes.

However, I soon grew tired of all the commands and almost felt like a hostage. The way he practically whipped me was a real disappointment. From day one, I was forced to perform all sorts of tasks within a very short timeframe. It was the middle of summer, a sweltering heat hung in the air, and the air was incredibly dusty. A little further on, a farmer with a large tractor was plowing an entire field. I'd never seen more dust; it hadn't rained in weeks. I nearly collapsed after an hour of intense digging when, on his advice; I was plowing the entire garden. My vision went black, and when I mentioned it, he scolded me for being a wimp. His physical advances were equally unpleasant. Things went from bad to worse; he tried to intimidate me, and when he realized I wasn't exactly receptive to his advances, the mood changed, and an aggressive atmosphere developed.

The management of the allotment complex was on his side because he was part of the new board. The old board would certainly have fully supported me; I had good contacts with them. I didn't have much to say anymore and had to comply with absurd demands that suddenly appeared, like removing weeds by a certain date, chemical pest control, removing plants due to pests—it went on and on. The litany of complaints seemed endless, never anything positive.

While my garden had truly become one of the most fertile, I let nature take its course, without bells and whistles like plastic tents, pesticides, or anything else.

Water was the best remedy. Every day I spent hours pumping water to water the plants. It worked fantastically, and the harvest was unprecedented.

I couldn't eat it all by myself. With all the vegetables and herbs being given away for free, I almost had more work. The fruit wasn't a problem. It was harvested effortlessly by others, stolen, actually. I only got to taste a very small amount of all the gooseberries, raspberries, strawberries, and other currants. From one day to the next, the entire strawberry field was picked clean, raspberries were removed, stem and all, or all the redcurrants had completely disappeared. I didn't live to see the gooseberries.

I had spent a small fortune on trees, plants, herbs, and tools.

It was always something, and when tools disappeared too, I got fed up. It started with a watering can that was nowhere to be found. Just to be able to quickly forget it to I took my bike to get a new one. It was a Saturday.

I was cycling on a remote road between deserted fields and farms when, from a distance, I heard a car approaching at a tremendous speed. It was an Audi, going so fast that I stopped and got off my bike to hide between two trees. It roared past at an absurdly high speed. Buying a watering can had almost cost me my life.

Sometime later, I found the watering can again. It was at another neighbor's, the one from the adjacent vegetable garden on the other side, in a large, closed container with tools. When he wasn't there, I plucked up the courage to lift the lid and, to my great surprise, saw the missing watering can lying there.

Except for a few friends with whom I often gardened there and whom I had met there, the atmosphere became increasingly grim. One of the guild members who owned the land told me I wasn't allowed to drink so much water because of the water bill. It continued, but it was the tap in the restroom building, not the water pump in the garden.

Surprised, I decided to stop using the restroom altogether. It was absurd, how much a little water cost, less than a euro per cubic meter. A glass of water, not even a cent.

Without any way to cool down, I cycled home on a scorching day on a bike with broken gears. The new one my foster family had promised me wasn't coming through; they preferred to give it to asylum seekers. I had to cross the road in a very high gear, which I couldn't do due to exhaustion. This caused me to fall and I couldn't get up.

I felt a terrible pain in my heart, as I lay there, completely exhausted. A group of cyclists passed by on the other side of the otherwise deserted road. They just kept cycling, having seen me fall—it was almost inevitable. Finally, a car stopped, a friendly man got out, and helped me up. I walked home, stumbling along.

I just made it the last two kilometers to my house, only to completely collapse at home. The first day after the accident, I was completely incapacitated and lay motionless in bed for twenty-four hours. A doctor friend advised me online to take it easy. It would be over in four weeks, and it was, to the letter. It had probably been a heart attack.

Slowly, I got back to my feet, and soon I had to go back to the allotment garden. The board had once again ordered some impossible task.

With an eye on the autumn and the coming spring, I had been busy for weeks, even months, taking cuttings from strawberry plants. No one had had so many strawberry cuttings, not in the entire complex. With all the plastic and chemical waste, they hadn't gotten very far. With a lot of herbs and other perennials and perennials, like strawberries, I wanted to reduce the number of labor-intensive annuals, which would immediately mean less work for spring. And I succeeded.

I had a beautiful layout, and the garden was starting to take shape. Day in, day out, I worked. Until the board and the man next to me became even more annoying, dangerous actually, I was threatened and forced to cancel my membership; I had no other choice.

My foster father had often gone to that garden, always when I wasn't there. As soon as he saw me, he immediately turned around. Once, he started a conversation, even though I can't have normal conversations with him; he never had any intentions towards me. When my biological father was still alive, he was kept somewhat in line, as much as possible. After his death, my foster father regularly raged like a beast whenever I was around. One day, completely out of nowhere, I was thrown to the ground and kicked in the head, near my temple, and stomped on my back, which was already broken by his actions. He left me there for dead and fled something he never did. We didn't see him again for the rest of Sunday. I stumbled to my bed and lay there all day, half-conscious. The next day I went back to Maastricht. The man I regularly rode with looked at my bruised ear in astonishment; my roommate noticed it immediately as well. It had a huge impact. I didn't immediately consider the physical side of this dramatic event. Although it was probably the cause of problems that came my way afterward, a heavy blow to the head can cause temporary confusion, even a psychosis. The psychological side of it all, your own father, or so I thought at the time, treating you like that. It happened relatively shortly after my biological father's death. My foster father had seen his chance and taken revenge for something that had happened a few years earlier, when I had just turned twenty-one, something trivial. He continued to take revenge for another forty years, over nothing, until I finally distanced myself and decided he'd had enough chances; he wouldn't change anymore.

They visited my garden at Easter, without informing me or inviting me. I wasn't invited at Christmas either, shortly after

Richard's death. Almost no one close to me, except my foster mother, had offered genuine condolences. They hadn't even visited me. I'd been alone after his death. Being alone at Christmas always hurts, especially then. Luckily, a friend took me along; I wasn't completely alone. Easter was the same story. It hurts when they're so mean as to go to your vegetable garden without your knowledge. They weren't even allowed in there. A quick phone call and I would have gone anyway. They tried to take over my identity in every way, destroying everything I built. They never engaged in conversation, as if I wasn't allowed to have an opinion, which wasn't the case. It was only their own warped opinions that prevailed, and with them, they tried to control my life.

And then to know that Richard and I always tried to help them with everything. They were often full of prejudices; they talked about me but never with me. They thought they knew everything, while they were usually completely wrong. They took those stories to authorities who believed them, which I then had to fight for decades, which wasn't easy.

The dog had also been in the garden, which was absolutely against the rules. There were dog tracks everywhere, truly disgusting. The thought of a dog urinating on my plants was unbearable.

All the work and investment had been for nothing, and to further corner me, I was forced to hand over the property as vacant land, bare of plants. This was a difficult task for me, without a car—which I had gotten rid of because of all the vandalism.

Since Richard's death, I've been nothing but harassed. You'd think people would have a little compassion, especially since I had to care for him largely on my own for ten years when he was ill, much longer, in fact. The opposite was true. In many ways, my life was made much more difficult than it already was. It seemed as if they saw their chance to take revenge, how cruel and for God knows what. Fortunately, there were a few exceptions, and not everyone was like that, although family largely refrained.

I immediately protested about the "clean" handover and threatened to call the police. I was completely fed up with it, especially the disrespect with which I was treated, which was actually abuse. After my threat to call the police, the problem was quickly resolved. Thanks to my warning, they quickly concluded they would find someone to take over the garden. The next day, they came to pick up the key. There was no time for me to retrieve anything from the garden. All the work had been for nothing; I couldn't even retrieve the tools.

These were all diabolical events. Lying and cheating won't get you anywhere. One day you'll be exposed, falling into the pit you tried to dig for someone else. What happened was all very unfair. In retrospect, I'm glad to be freed from the arduous task, not suited for a woman alone. Being able to find something positive in events is crucial. They had been trying to undermine Richard and me for years, literally, and it wasn't just my vegetable garden that was destroyed. During my husband's illness and after his death, they targeted my car and once loosened a wheel. They vandalized his grave, which I considered almost the worst part. This and many other events were decisive. I was done enough. This aggression had to stop.

I distanced myself and, as if that weren't enough, was also called a pathetic, lonely woman when I was just a widow—one of the many examples of how they tried to humiliate me. The only person I could still respect was my foster mother; she was right in the thick of it, and has since passed away, too awful for words.

I had cared for Richard all alone for eight years when he was ill. Although the GP sent some caregivers remotely, they ultimately said they couldn't do much, which wasn't true. Due to a lack of medical help, he spiraled further into psychosis. Time and again, I went to the GP's office to ask for help, but each time, my request was rejected. Only after seven years did the GP himself come to investigate, presumably after being pointed out his mistakes.

Day in, day out, I spent years with a terminally ill man, unable to move. It wasn't taken seriously, even though psychosis is one of the most serious conditions you can have. This was mainly due to family members who, behind the scenes, blocked help. My family did nothing, even though some of them worked in healthcare. They all looked the other way. I had suffered quite a few blows, both literally and figuratively, because of the situation that had arisen. There was hardly any help, and they blamed me, which was completely pointless. They judged something they knew nothing about. From a distance, my family just yelled, called authorities, and blamed me. It was absolutely pointless, and they refused to talk with me about it. At least it was officially acknowledged afterward that it wasn't my fault. Very nice, but the consequences of this disaster, you could call it, were irreversible and are still palpable daily.

And it got worse, the damage to my car increased in severity. That beautiful car that Richard and I had saved for so long; it was our hobby. How dare you, I thought to myself, I really needed that car, if only because of Richard's illness, for example, to transport his wheelchair. The windshield, once like new, was completely smeared with dog poop and sand, it was covered in scratches and dents, and I had to have it repaired. Sand had also gotten into the engine, causing damage to one of the injectors, an expensive 'joke'. The car was scratched several times. Every morning I had to check if some scoundrel had messed with my car again. And why, I kept wondering. Sometimes there were notes under my car. After Richard's death, things got even worse, as if I didn't have enough to worry about. They weren't just targeting my car, but the grave as well; vandalism happened again and again.

I was hit from behind, and the car eventually had to be scrapped. I tried to have it repaired, but to no avail.

The vandalism at the grave was almost worse, or even worse. Every time I went there, something happened. The original temporary monument had been vandalized with brute force, and it didn't stop there. It was clear to me who the perpetrator was; he continued to annoy me for years, standing at my window at night, doing the craziest things. What happened in the vegetable garden is also directly related; the same perpetrator was behind all this.

Someone in my family was severely abused throughout her childhood. It started when I was four and she was three. She blames me for it, and that's unfair. The perpetrator never wanted to make things right, even unfairly, because I've been a victim of this my whole life. It's an unstoppable emotional rollercoaster, a dangerous woman because she can't control her emotions and react very aggressively. None of it was my fault, but it was a fate I've had to bear for decades.

I'm trying to put it behind me, including my contact with them. They think they have authority over you because they're family, which of course makes no sense. They're people without common sense who often lash out and cause trouble everywhere. It's best to stay away.

And then there's something else: the key to my house. I've had cylinders replaced many times, but the key specialist the landlord hires always manages to keep one through that same person. This is, of course, not the intention. Because of this, my foster father recently came into my house with that same man, the key specialist. I have plenty of evidence of this. They sometimes do such strange things that they can no longer control them, and they always use my so-called (incorrect) diagnosis as an excuse. My half-sister, who is completely crazy herself, calls the authorities behind my back and then comes up with some story about needing a key, which is false and not allowed. I explained this story to the landlord once, but after that, they sent the same man again, and I had to pay again, and again, he withheld a key. Recently, I had a standing appointment, because this makes it almost impossible for me to get out.

Making appointments is another opportunity for them to break in, and also a sign that they even know when I have appointments. They're terribly compulsive people; the internet and phone are much less secure than people think. I don't want to bother the landlord with these problems anymore. That's why I'm leaving it alone, for now, because in a year I'll probably get new doors and window frames, and then it might be solved. It might be, because they'll probably come up with another trick if this continues. And it's always been this way. They vandalized my car, Richard's grave, broke into things, and committed robberies. They have to live with everything they've done, and that's even more. I'm housebound because of this, and for the same reason, I've been able to write a book, and this isn't the last one. By not having a car, I've been able to save a lot of money. It's not nice when something like this happens, yet God will always protect you, and every event usually has a positive side, no matter how strange that may sound. Some things you can't change or you can't change immediately. In that case, the best thing is to accept it and pray for better times. People with the technical ability can see everything on your screen. This can be protection, but it can also end up in the wrong hands. Resistance and trying to solve such problems is, of course, very good, even if it has its limits. That's when you must hand it over to God. You can never control everything. It's best to surround yourself with as many good people as possible and stay as far away from bad people as possible, because they exist. Bad people exist. There is often something good to be found in everyone. Yet, evil, the devil, can prevail within a person, and you can't always neutralize the bad with the good.

Vegetables

*F*resh food is, of course, best; it contributes to good health, with vegetables taking center stage. Nothing is better for a person, although you naturally need a whole host of other nutrients. Besides, the way to a person's heart is through the stomach; healthy eating makes them feel better, contributes to their general well-being, and has healing properties, just like herbs.

In the 1930s, a German, Otto Warburg, won the Nobel Prize for a method for naturally curing cancer. However, it wasn't given much attention, as the pharmaceutical industry couldn't profit from it.

Nevertheless, I want to delve into the essence of it here, a medical hypothesis that has long been proven: the connection between the body's pH and the development of cancer cells. When the human body's pH is too low, it's called acidification, which is unhealthy and can be dangerous. The perfect pH is 7.365. A difference of 0.5 makes the body stop functioning, that's how precise it is. A cancer cell is essentially fueled by sugars. It's common knowledge how unhealthy sugar is. Even with too much fruit, you have to be careful, not just to prevent cancer.

There are many other conditions you can develop due to an unhealthy lifestyle.

Stress is unhealthy. Excessive stress releases substances in the body that can threaten your health, especially if there's excessive stress for a prolonged period.

The same applies to unhealthy food. Regarding nutrition, there's a direct link between the body's pH and the food in question.

Each food can be assigned a specific pH value. I'll give a few examples from memory to make it easier to understand. There used to be tables online to illustrate this, but these have almost all disappeared. Censorship is the problem. People shouldn't know about it. The WEF wants chemical treatments, fast-food chains, and certainly no herbal remedies. It shouldn't be too natural, and above all, it should generate a lot of money. That's the real conspiracy. A cancer cell cannot survive in a healthy body and dies within 24 hours if the body's pH is correct. For vegetables, the average pH is usually 8 or 9, meaning that eating them helps maintain a good balance in cases of acidification. Vegetables and nuts are just about the only foods with such a very high pH; most other foods tend to have a lower pH. For example, the pH of a hamburger or cola is much lower, two or three, meaning that eating them has a direct impact on well-being and health. While one occasion isn't a problem, long-term exposure, or frequent consumption of unhealthy meals, has a much greater impact than many people realize.

Tanja Groen

There were many moments in my life when I thought: This story needs to be told.

After Tanja Groen's abduction in the early 1990s, another reason emerged. I was also a member of Circumflex, the student association in Maastricht that she wanted to join when she disappeared during orientation. Not only that, but she also wanted to study Health Sciences. The path she wanted to take resonated with part of my past, although I hadn't lived in Maastricht for quite some time at the time this all happened.

Her roommate was named Bram; they both rented a room in the same building in Gronsveld, a small town near Maastricht. Bram probably originally came from the Uden area, where I once lived. He also wanted to join Circumflex and participated in orientation, although he wasn't there the night of her disappearance.

She was never seen again after leaving the student association building late one Tuesday evening, alone, by bicycle, into the dark night. Gronsveld is about six kilometers from Maastricht. It was around midnight when she wanted to cycle back to her room—at least, that was the assumption, and she had told people at Circumflex that she was going there.

That's probably how it happened, although in retrospect, it might not have been her immediate destination. People in the area heard screams about two hours later, somewhere along the route she must have cycled, near Gronsveld.

There was a considerable time lag between the time they saw her cycling away from the student society and the time they heard the scream—two hours, while it's only about a half-hour bike ride.

Members of the student society had offered to join her for a bit of the ride, or even all the way, to Gronsveld. They felt it irresponsible for her to cycle all the way alone in the dark. She had waved it off.

"I can do that!" she might have thought.

"I'm a strong girl!"

Or perhaps she had other plans, which could also have been a secret rendezvous. We don't know; little has been learned about it so far.

The screaming must have had something to do with it. You don't often hear someone screaming in the middle of the night in a deserted area on a route where it later turned out someone, namely Tanja Groen, must have disappeared. And it was indeed the night she disappeared. About two hours after she left Herbenusstraat in Maastricht on her bicycle, someone was heard screaming very loudly.

In principle, she could have reached the point where people heard this from their homes in less than half an hour with her bicycle, but it was two hours later than would logically be expected.

It's therefore possible that she went somewhere else after leaving the club. Perhaps there was a budding romance; perhaps she already had more contacts in Maastricht than initially suspected.

Wim S. could have been a possibility.

He eventually became a suspect in this disappearance and, during the summer of the disappearance, was staying at a campsite not far from Maastricht, in Valkenburg, a bit further from Maastricht than Gronsveld. Tanja Groen was also staying there, coincidentally, with her family, probably looking for a room.

Almost no information about Wim S. exists online anymore. This was different some time ago. Back then, it was still possible to find that he worked at Mora Snacks branches in Eindhoven, Maastricht, and possibly Brussels. This information has disappeared from the internet, as has a great deal of other information about this suspect in the Tanja Groen disappearance, a case that occurred about thirty years ago and has become a cold case. It received a great deal of publicity, mainly due to the efforts of Peter R. de Vries, a crime reporter. It likely cost him his life, or at least he is no longer alive. The assassination attempt on his life may have been related to this case.

Wim S.

im S. was suspected of several murders, one of which he was convicted for because sufficient evidence was found. In conversations with a fellow inmate, he confessed to ten murders and also claimed to be the perpetrator of Tanja Groen's disappearance, "that girl from Maastricht," as he called her.

Wim S. had also crossed my path about ten years earlier, although I didn't know who he was at the time. He wanted to meet me, whom I didn't accept, but I can imagine he might have approached Tanja Groen in the same way. She must have gotten off her bike somewhere, though its unclear where, and it's certainly not something to joke about; it's a serious matter.

It wouldn't have made sense for someone to take her, abuse her, or something similar, and then drop her off again an hour later on the same route, causing her to scream. That would have been an illogical scenario. Someone who abuses someone will want to cover their tracks; that's how things go, even I know that much about crime.

What also seems logical to me is that young children are used because they can't, or have a harder time, recounting the story. Tanja Groen was no longer a child, but a young girl.

For starters, you have plenty of reason to start screaming at everyone immediately when something so awful happens to a woman, not just two hours later. Moreover, it's illogical that she would be put back on the road after any form of abuse.

It's just as possible that people waited for her somewhere and pretended to be members of the student association. During such an introduction, you're constantly being dragged around in vans, a kind of prank that got out of hand. That wouldn't have been the first time.

Therefore, it's possible that criminals waited for her somewhere in a van and pretended to be members of the student association. It seems clear to me that whoever contributed to her disappearance was aware of the introduction, and it also seems logical to assume that Wim S. didn't act alone.

Making a young woman disappear on your own seems very difficult.

I happen to know this because my half-sister once attacked me at home on a Friday evening, just before Carnival, when I was alone. The doorbell rang; it was around seven o'clock in the evening. She had been acting annoying earlier that day and had a very frightening look in her eyes. At first, we didn't answer the door, but this time I did. I shouldn't have; it was clear she hadn't come for a pleasant visit. Her eyes were burning, and once again she wanted to use me as a target to vent her aggression, and even worse, she wanted to literally finish me off; that was very clear. It was as if she finally wanted to turn decades of pent-up hatred into an irreversible act. She'd tried it before; her completely unwarranted hatred of me was unprecedented.

At first, she kept kicking the glass door, endlessly and very hard. I was afraid she'd smash the glass, but I'd long since learned my lesson not to just open it.

Because she kicked so hard, I opened it anyway, mainly to prevent the glass from being smashed. I shouldn't have done that; she wanted to overpower me and gain entry to the house, probably to smash the place to pieces, like she'd done at my foster parents' house. She must have needed a fix; she'd probably been addicted to hard drugs for about thirty years at that point. She had managed to hide it well, partly due to very poor communication. Very bad, you can see that now, or you could say back then, it's always bad. We humans are communicative beings; it's not for nothing that we have highly developed senses and the ability to speak and listen. The fact that many people only use ten percent of their brain capacity is demonstrably clear here; I, at least, was being deprived of a lot of information. Dangerous, life-threatening in this case.

I was at my wits' end. She kept pushing against the door, which was now half open, and I could barely hold her back. With great difficulty, I managed to fish an umbrella from another corner of the hall, and with that, I managed to chase her away. I was in shock and watched her disappear into the darkness; I'll never forget that image.

What I'm trying to say is that I know what can happen when a woman resists, because if you're threatened with being taken against your will, you resist; that seems quite logical to me. The forces released can be similar; you can hardly handle that alone. Moreover, there are other reasons why I suspect Wim S. didn't act alone, and I know, from hearsay, probably also where she might have met: in the city itself, near the station. That seems to me the most likely version of this very dramatic event, which ultimately stemmed from lust. Jealousy is also a form of lust; not wishing someone else well. And you can bet you'll never have anything yourself if you're like that. It's a devilish attitude that never got anyone anywhere. Everything is temporary, and nothing lasts. You have to change that to avoid burning in hell for the rest of your life.

All things considered, the most logical option is that she had an appointment somewhere in Maastricht, perhaps in a hotel, and didn't tell her fellow students, possibly out of shame, subconsciously sensing something wasn't right.

She might have left after an hour or so, and someone might have waited for her on the route.

The appointment was also meant to determine the time she would return "home." That's how criminals operate, it seems to me.

A sane person devises plans to achieve something positive.

This case, however, is devising plans to carry out a kidnapping, which, of course, they want to keep as far from public view as possible. A sinister plan, anything but healthy. So, she might have had a date with someone very late that evening, after attending the student party, perhaps around 11:30.

Or someone wanted to see her to know what time she would be cycling back, so they could have some idea of her whereabouts. Cell phones weren't around back then.

The fact is that there was a suspect in the picture who was supposedly deceased, which I don't believe either. He supposedly murdered several girls, he once confessed in conversations with a fellow inmate, and committed ten murders. At the time of this confession, he was incarcerated for one of the murders, was later sentenced to TBS (Tenure-Based Treatment) and then spent some time in a specific institution—you guessed it.

It's also a fact that this Wim S. was staying with his family at a campsite in Valkenburg the summer before all this happened, where Tanja Groen and her family were also staying at the time. He may also have been there, or still is, at the time of the induction; something is known about that as well. I know of people who may have cooperated, voluntarily or not, that they may have stayed at a specific hotel.

It's hard to imagine, but it's quite possible she had arranged to meet him of her own free will.

Wim S. was terrified that his wife would find out about what he had committed. From an audio recording made of him by Peter R. de Vries, you can gather that being overly friendly and nice can be so overwhelming that a woman could fall for it, especially during a hazing ritual. In fact, you should always be vigilant at such times; often, there's more to it.

SV Circumflex

*I*t's certain that it wasn't just an introduction, but a hazing experience. Circumflex was already a fraternity where, as a health scientist, you felt a bit out of place. It was mainly law and economics students who joined. Almost exclusively, after I had canceled my membership three years earlier to complete my doctorate and that didn't change overnight.

They used to have a completely different approach, before a group of law and economics students revived the association and restored all sorts of old, almost lost, student traditions. It was once an association for everyone attending higher professional education (HBO) or university in Maastricht. That changed after the takeover; there was a selection committee, and Bram ultimately didn't make the cut that much was clear. At one point, there was even a manager in the pub downstairs, so we had our own bar. At that time, there was a bit of a battle between two student associations in Maastricht, Tragos and Circumflex. Both wanted to claim the title of student corps, and sometimes they even raided each other. Some fraternity or other would unexpectedly invade the rival association. Many Tragos members attended Hotel Management School in Maastricht and, for that reason alone, could never have become the Maastricht corps. Etiquette was highly valued at Circumflex; the norms and values of decency had to be observed; if not, you were called out on it. It was an instructive time. Without the association's support, I would never have succeeded in obtaining my doctorate. You no longer felt alone as a student in a room on the third floor; there was always a place you could go to meet fellow students. Student life is often romanticized, but who hasn't heard the term "poor student"? It's hard work, and if you perform below par, you're easily dismissed. Circumflex had its own canteen, where you could get a delicious meal for a small price in the evenings. It took place at a fixed time, with everyone sitting together at long tables. I was a member of the canteen committee for a while and, as such, regularly found myself busy in the kitchen with pots and pans. I also dated one of the board members but wasn't a member of a fraternity, which was a personal choice.

The beer cantus was a centuries-old tradition that was revived in Maastricht under the auspices of Circumflex. Students sang songs from a traditional songbook, the codex. A beer cantus was usually held in a special location, the very location itself oozing with authenticity and tradition. A unique experience you'll never forget: The beer is poured from watering cans, and you're only allowed to take a sip at the command of the president—who chairs the "meeting" with his entire board. Whether you have to finish the glass in one go depends on a number of factors: for ad libidum, one sip is enough; at ad fundum, the entire glass must be emptied at once. The room is filled with long tables and benches to accommodate everyone, and the evening is filled with songs sung standing up. The president indicates when everyone must stand or sit down. Sometimes special tasks must be fulfilled, and you can only hope you don't end up being the loser, or the unlucky one. When the president indicates a particular song, he mentions the page in the codex, for example, 365. He then mentions the full number, in this case three hundred and sixty-five, and then the individual digits: Three, six, five. He then reverses it: Five, six, three. It may sound strange, but all in all, it's an informative and, above all, unforgettable evening, brimming with old traditions. Nostalgia is the right word, and you could even call it typically Belgian.

The student association received a real boost after the group of friends - one of whom came from Belgium, where studied for a while at a centuries-old university - took over the place. The beer cantus was an old Belgian custom.

These are very fond memories; they can make people jealous. Jealousy can stem from feeling excluded. Close-knit groups of people, in particular, can fuel this feeling in outsiders. They often only see the positive aspects, in this case, for example, of student life; the hard work a student has to put in every day gets less attention, creating a romanticized image. Obtaining a doctorate in, in my case, a very demanding medical field, is certainly no easy feat.

Another example of a tradition the student association maintained was the presentation of a certificate after successfully completing hazing. The year I received this document, certified with a wax seal, the reception was held in the university's corona room. I had never been in that room before; I can still remember it being a particularly luxuriously decorated space with lots of red and white. But you can imagine that they already had a COVID room back then—it was in the 1980s.

Tanja Groen was therefore something of an odd duck among the generally right-wing students, while health scientists were generally quite left-leaning. I don't think the field of study as such still exists.

In that sense, I was also an exception, a right-wing health scientist who believed that people should take much more responsibility for their own health and be pampered much less, only when absolutely necessary. At the time, I didn't even realize how much everything revolved around money. Health Sciences is a holistic program; the human being is seen as a whole; body and mind go together. A healthy mind in a healthy body is the ultimate goal. Maastricht University's educational system was also unique; they used the seven-step approach, with problem-solving learning at its core. You start with the problem, analyze it, and then use that to find the information you need. Memorizing entire books or studying them from cover to cover isn't necessary; the course material is essentially reversed.

That works to a certain extent and is certainly useful. This way of studying teaches you to solve problems in a much broader sense; it's applicable to almost anything. Once you've mastered this method, you can much more easily study other fields. To a certain extent, because when I started studying Human Movement Sciences, a major within the spectrum, it became clear that basic knowledge was indeed very important. Soon, the old-fashioned anatomy and physiology lectures were brought back.

Tanja Groen doesn't know which field within Health Sciences she wanted to study; perhaps she didn't know yet. During hazing, you're put to the test, that's for sure, and it can be educational, too, and it can be draining.

A little moral support from someone you know from a completely different perspective can be a welcome change at such a time. In that sense, it's understandable that Tanja Groen might have arranged to meet Wim S., the serial killer, about who little was known at the time. He might have acted as a kind of father figure. Such figures, especially through excessive kindness, know how to win the hearts of naive, unsuspecting girls.

Although, in retrospect, things turned out completely differently, she couldn't have been more wrong. Imagine the value of human judgment. She was the first in her family to pursue a university education, and her parents may also have been too trusting, unaware of the dangers that can lurk when a child moves out of town. She may have had a very sheltered upbringing, which seems logical to me. Suddenly being thrown in at the deep end, far from your parental home, can have quite an impact.

The fact is that Wim S. was definitely involved, my husband told me so on his deathbed. He had information about this case, and I have no reason to doubt it, although I was quite taken aback when he told me all this. It was the moment when, through a foundation established by Peter R. de Vries, a million euros was promised to anyone who could provide information that could solve the case. It got my husband talking, even though he was barely able to do so at the time due to near-total physical paralysis; he was very ill. The money probably wasn't even the motivation; the publicity was probably much more important.

It was immensely sad; talking to him had become very difficult.

Once the truth was out on the subject, he couldn't speak at all for weeks. After a month or so, his speech returned a tiny bit. Not long after, he passed away. He couldn't provide many details.

Family

During my investigation into this case, I discovered that Wim S. had literally crossed my path once, in the summer of 1984, when I briefly worked for Mora Snacks in Maastricht to earn some extra money for my studies.

It was puzzling that he had moved all the way from Geldrop to work there, while Mora Snacks also had a branch in Eindhoven, almost a stone's throw from his home. The distance between Maastricht and Geldrop is about a hundred kilometers, quite unusual for someone to travel such a distance for a job on an assembly line in a factory.

He was working next to me and at some point approached me for an appointment.

At that time, I had just moved into an apartment above a general practitioner's office in the center of Maastricht, not far from Herbenusstraat, incidentally, where the student association was located at the time of Tanja Groen's disappearance. I was going to share the apartment with a friend who already lived there. She was originally from Acht, near Eindhoven, and was very good friends with someone also from Acht, who had also been the neighbor of a friend of my foster father.

The friendship between her and her best friend had been strained for some reason, which meant a vacancy had opened up in the apartment where they had lived together until recently.

The young woman I had moved in with forced me to help remove a layer of cement from the living room floor. This layer had once been applied to the wooden floor, which was carpeted, to level it. My roommate wanted to remove it and then renovate the wooden floor, which she preferred. The carpet was indeed in need of replacement, I have to admit.

Still, this was a rental, and it was a hell of a job. When I came home in the evening from a full day of working on the assembly line, I had to go back to work. She'd been sitting on the floor all day and had grown thirty square centimeters, all very strange.

And especially absurd, how she then kicked me out of the house, and even worse, how she completely smeared me to all my friends, whom I lost as a result; they believed her stories.

I didn't accept Wim S.'s request to meet up with him. It felt so bad that I quit my summer job the day after he even followed me as I tried to cycle home. Shortly before, a team leader from Mora Snacks had very conspicuously dropped a so-called Parker pen into the meat snack batter while I was standing next to him. Perhaps he smelled something bad or knew something about it. Because it wasn't just a pan of meat batter or ragout they used to make the meat snack of; it was a pan the size of three enormous containers, meters high and meters deep, into which the pen fell. He was standing on a high stepladder when it happened. There was a kind of railing around the large, round meat snack pan, which even had a huge mixer attached to it, ensuring that not only the meat but also, in this case, the skewer was ground. He didn't bat an eye when it happened and didn't even react, making no effort to retrieve the skewer. I thought it was quite abnormal and decided never to eat that kind of meat snack again. In retrospect, it was a kind of 'warning'. The team leader had probably gotten wind of what was happening on the work floor.

The world is full of dangers, and now that I realize all this, because I've thought about it deeply, it almost hurts me more than I realized then. Of course, I found myself in a terrible situation, and that had a huge impact for years to come, but the idea that someone wanted to harm me in this way is painful, even wanting to kill my own father, because he never honestly admitted he was my foster father. That's something I had to figure out for myself. Apparently, he only took on that task for money.

Richard even told me that he had ordered Tanja Groen's disappearance. Not just me, but everyone around me had to suffer, and I still don't know why. Of course, it's incomprehensible that people are so stupid as to murder others and think they'll go free. These are such serious facts that people endlessly search for the perpetrators. Eliminating those around them who have information is somewhat understandable, though it's mainly a sign of unparalleled stupidity. It's all disrespectful and deeply criminal. Some people, who are certainly exponents of this, find it equally disrespectful that I'm writing this down. However, I'm allowed to stand up for myself, and these events, in which I had no part or involvement, which were directed against me completely without my knowledge, have had a profound impact on my life. If you analyze the matter meticulously, you can conclude that it's all about my biological parents and the fact that I grew up with foster parents, a financial issue—it's too awful to put into words that it could be the reason for killing your own child. Germanic customs certainly play a role in the background; otherwise, you wouldn't entrust your five-year-old daughter to an orphanage known for it. It's fortunate that Het Ronde Huis had just been demolished; otherwise, I might not have been alive at all.

First of all, I'm loyal to Circumflex. Thanks to my membership, I graduated. Relaxation is important; I also wanted to investigate this out of respect for Tanja Groen's parents. Moreover, the crimes committed against me were, and still are, so serious that there was no other choice; this had to stop, no matter what. How sick are you as a father? I was married to Richard. It was my good fortune that Richard couldn't bring himself to do it, although he certainly tried, and not insignificantly.

Richard also knew my grandfather Steenbakkers, my foster mother's father. He was a butcher and owned his own butcher shop and slaughterhouse. My great-grandfather was also a butcher, although he also owned a café and basket-making business. Both were excellent butchers. My great-grandfather's butcher shop closed not so long ago, but it existed for so long. It's a dying breed; supermarkets have taken over everything. The Steenbakkers family and Richard's ex-in-laws likely knew each other from a distant past. The building where the butcher shop was located may have once belonged to Richard's ex-father-in-law, and before that, a Shell gas station was located there.

There weren't many of them back then—I'm talking about the 1930s and 1940s, when very few people owned cars. Although my great-grandfather owned the café, the basket-making shop, and a butcher shop in Heeswijk, nearby Schijndel, where many Steenbakkers once lived, not only had brickworks but also, long ago, a Shell branch. All of this was within easy reach of 's-Hertogenbosch, not far from Vucht, where a group of people who had fled Indonesia lived for a long time shortly after the Second World War. Richard's ex-in-laws belonged to this group, although Richard's ex-father-in-law was Dutch by birth. So, this is a history that goes back a very long way. My grandmother, the wife of Jan Steenbakkers, died quite young after a life of very hard work, which was the case with a butcher's shop and a slaughterhouse, my foster mother, also knew everything about. Sometimes it seemed as if she had to keep everything running on her own, she had to work so hard. It wasn't just the business; she also had to care for the children, six of whom my grandfather had.

When my grandmother died, my grandfather, after a while, moved in with an acquaintance of my foster mother. He couldn't be alone, and my foster parents wouldn't take him in, even though he would have liked to.

That acquaintance of my foster mother was related to Richard's ex-mother-in-law. It's a small world, but I didn't know him then. It was years later, in the mid-nineties, that I met him, in a completely different setting, by the way.

The ex-mother-in-law turned out to be a lesbian, just like my grandfather's girlfriend. When he died, the two women moved in together. They were already related—though not by bloodline, but by marriage—and then even more so. It's a complicated story; I'd rather not mention too many names. Moreover, it felt completely out of place to me when all this happened, near the village where I grew up. I was studying and had been living somewhere else for about ten years at the time, only to return after graduating. However, I was very unaware of all the troubles and complications at the time; I had other things on my mind. I didn't meet Richard until much later. I vaguely remember seeing him at some family party around that time, but I certainly didn't meet him then. Moreover, I suspect he was in touch with friends and acquaintances of mine in Maastricht, where his paintings hung in a hotel near the station. Even then, there was a great deal of distance between him and me; I never met him there or became acquainted. These are all things I learned later. Many years later, in the mid-nineties, I met him when he had been admitted to the Institution, where I also spent some time. I probably took his place there in a certain unit. When I was admitted, it coincided with his departure to De Wijst social housing, not to be confused with De Weijst. It's a community next to the Institution, but as such, completely separate from it. De Wijst is, however, part of the Institution.

For the preceding weeks, I had been admitted to a secure unit due to my extremely poor physical condition at the time. Although I had no authorization for compulsory admission, it was voluntary, but it was for my own protection that I stayed in a secure unit, P2. It sends shivers down the spines of many people familiar with the scene, especially now, and even now. I don't remember much about those weeks in P2, except that I barely left the unit, only with supervision, and that I had conversations with a pastor. I slowly recovered and was transferred to Springelbeek 2, presumably taking over from Richard, who was then moving to De Wijst in Gemert. I never met him on the grounds of the institution during that time; it wasn't until a few years later that I first met him.

I got an apartment near De Wijst and went there for coffee with a friend.

About a year after I rented that apartment, I went there for the first time. I don't remember exactly, it was a long time ago.

That friend lived around the corner from me, and we often went out together.

After some time, and that might have been a year later, I met Richard for the first time. He was sleeping a lot then, which must have been one reason he hadn't been in the living room much earlier.

I was startled by his appearance; he did nothing but pace around the room, stiff with pills, talking about the difficult situation he'd found himself in after a divorce. About a year or two later, I started seeing him more often. Towards the end of the nineties, after a year of dating, I moved in with him.

My foster father had wanted revenge for something very trivial that happened when I was a teenager. Puberty had also been a difficult time, and the inheritance issue was lurking in the background, something I only became aware of many years later.

All things considered, he might have contacted my roommate for all these distorted reasons. Completely out of the blue, she suddenly became very unpleasant towards me. Because of her, I lost all my friends. Finding another room so close to the start of the new academic year wasn't easy either, and I had to manage it all on my own, including financially.

Being thwarted in every way by my own family, my whole life, has defined my life and is indescribably painful, especially because I'm quite the opposite, helping each other as family members. It took me a long time to understand how mean they were; they did everything just to elevate themselves. It was truly awful when you're like that. After everything they did to me, I still almost feel sorry for them. My mother wasn't like that, although it took a long time for her to take a stand. If she had an opinion of her own, it was mercilessly punished.

Hence that dreadful job at Mora Snacks, so I could at least earn some extra money to pay for my studies. Years later, Circumflex offered a solution. When I joined, I met a lot of new people and was able to leave behind the left-wingers I'd been friends with until then, and had met during my time at the Mikojel Academy. Not that that time wasn't also very valuable; in some ways, it was incredibly educational, all those creative fields and the opportunities for personal development. Friendship, however, is something else entirely.

My old roommate had also had a summer job, but the removal of the cement floor hadn't worked out, and she too eventually had to move out. You could almost say it was her fault, although it's not all that simple, and that theory doesn't always hold water.

A few years earlier, I was studying creative therapy at the Mikojel Academy in Sittard. Behind my back, my foster father had been in contact with the extremely corrupt landlord I had there for the first six months, the worst slumlord ever. I found that contact very strange, and I only understand it now. Even then, he was working behind the scenes to ruin my life. What kind of father are you? A horror, if you ask me, even though he still manages to keep so much hidden from the outside world, and there are many people who still can't believe these kinds of stories.

It's all true, I can assure you. You couldn't even make something like that up; that's what it takes.

It's all far too bizarre; he can put on a very good front. Because he often tries to be in the spotlight, I couldn't avoid contact with him for a long time. He was always there when family was around, and even when they weren't, he made sure of that, so compulsive. It often led to problems, his way of thinking and acting—often far too emotional, not thinking things through first, and few healthy ideas. He has fewer bad sides, although in these kinds of cases, you can't just cancel out all the issues, which is, incidentally, his way of thinking.

That was his way of doing things, never talking to me, only talking about me—truly awful. My half-sister and foster sister have picked up a lot from him. They think they know everything about you but only ever hear one side of the story, and they profit from that; they have little sense of good intentions. It's mainly about money, money, and more money, and not to forget, things. What they've done is extremely unlawful, also due to libel and slander. For example, they published a book about me, based on stolen medical records and diaries my foster father kept, which is already quite sick in itself. It showed once again how carelessly he handles personal information, to put it mildly.

How sick are you as a parent? It's absolutely unacceptable to just throw someone's medical information out into the open. It's also highly unethical.

The book may have been related to the compensation claim discussed earlier, but to make matters worse, I haven't received a cent of it. Honestly, I've never received any money from family.

Very small amounts that were more like a reimbursement to me than a gift.

That's not fair enough; my half-sister has received a considerable amount of money from them over the years.

With that, she was able to undermine Richard and me.

The Canadian who received eight billion in compensation from the company, an unbelievable sum, was possibly my cousin posing as my brother. He called me around the time the incident occurred, claiming I had a brother, but he didn't say who. In any case, I haven't seen a cent of that money; he's not my brother, and I barely have any contact with him, as has always been the case.

However, I did take Risperdal wrongly for decades and suffered many complaints from the terrible side effects. It's no wonder that the aforementioned sum, though exorbitant, was paid out to someone as compensation. I always assumed a patient would have received it. This money may belong to me, or at least a significant portion of it. I'm the one who was wrongly forced to take the drug for twenty-five years and became seriously ill from it. Moreover, I still suffer from the terrible side effects, and this intense, prolonged episode in my life has destroyed almost everything I've tried to build, including my social life. My foster father is a man who has difficulty forgiving and often gets into arguments. He's a dangerous man who, out of nowhere, threw me to the ground one day, stomped on my back, and kicked me in the head. That's where my illness began. After a temporary break from studies, I graduated but then completely collapsed. This was after years of abuse at home, especially on weekends, for no apparent reason, out of pure jealousy, really. In hindsight, I understand it better, although what they did to me is far from condoning, and I myself did nothing wrong.

If I ever tried to "strike back," usually not literally, it was out of self-defense.

My foster mother couldn't help it; she was also a victim and didn't even survive, just like Richard, she was the same story. Innocent, really, completely pressured and cornered, utterly intimidated.

Hardly a day goes by that I don't think about it, Tanja Groen. I try to dig into my memories again, about the city I loved so much and where I haven't visited often since graduating. Richard told me on his deathbed how it all happened: Wim S. did it, on my foster father's orders.

I could go on for ages about this. I myself had nothing to do with it, although my foster father also always did everything to cast suspicion on me. He wanted to kill me, and still does. My half-sister isn't doing much better; in fact, she's the victim of an honor killing, revenge my foster father wanted to take on my foster mother. My half-sister was severely abused and mistreated as a child; as was my foster mother, though they both managed to hide this for a long time. That in itself indicates how serious it all was. That man is insane.

Out of jealousy, my half-sister completely destroyed my life and, for that very reason, had a book written about me, full of lies, based on stolen medical records and stolen diary entries from my foster father, who kept a diary about me, very ill, and all falsely. It's a shameful book full of libel. They played a part in Richard's death, at least by blocking help, probably also by poisoning him; that he was poisoned is a fact. After his death, my car was vandalized, and my half-sister desecrated his grave. I was on my own everywhere, no one actually helped me, and I also had to process my grief largely on my own. They had vilified me everywhere, wrongly, and I hadn't done anything wrong.

Left-wing extremists blamed Circumflex for my illness, which was completely absurd. It was precisely because of the student association that I was ultimately able to graduate. They judge far too quickly and are poor communicators.

It's all too horrific, and of course they say it's not true, but it is. I've researched this for decades; these are my findings, and Richard has told me a lot about it. It's probably related to an inheritance from my biological father that all this came about. They ran off with the money, and I didn't see a cent of it. I've certainly found a lot of evidence for that. That I was an heir is also certain, as is the fact that there was something to be divided up. It's all corroborated by evidence. The fact that he was possibly very wealthy could certainly have played a role. They were also angry with Verstappen, the man who founded the Human Movement Sciences program wasn't a nice guy either. They promised the world and didn't keep their promises. That Human Movement Sciences program was incredibly tough. I barely managed to survive. A fellow student named Akeline, also from Uden, who also took almost the same path.

She didn't survive; she sadly passed away some time ago, after a very difficult life full of problems.

And then there are most likely a few more patients from the institution who were unintentionally involved in these criminal acts, absolutely beyond words. I was taken by the head nurse from De Wijst for a weekend trip to Maastricht; you can imagine how corrupt it was, almost unimaginable. When I discovered that, I really felt like I'd been completely ripped off. Who would do something like that? Because that was possibly the weekend Tanja disappeared; it's possible she was at the hotel that night where the group of patients led by the head nurse was staying. I initially assumed I was still admitted when she disappeared, but I can't quite remember; it was a long time ago. It means I might already be living in the apartment at the time, though I'm still unsure about that. I certainly didn't know Richard yet, but I do know that for sure. He had paintings hanging in the hotel, which is why they went there—that was at least one reason.

It's possible that Bram must have been involved somehow, the roommate who might have deliberately been absent that evening so Tanja wouldn't be alone otherwise. He has the same last name as the head nurse, so that could be a warning sign. The traffic light is amber, let's put it that way—not exactly red, but certainly not green either, speaking of green.

My half-sister often went to Maastricht in the nineties with all her lying stories and attempts to destroy me even further. Her hatred arose when she was three or four, and I was five, because my foster father abused her almost daily. He always said, "Take Carmen as an example!" She had a completely different personality than me, and she was also slightly mentally challenged, probably from all the abuse. After everything she put me through, it's very difficult for me not to develop a deep dislike for her. Ultimately, though, it wasn't her fault when you're so severely abused. Because that's a fact, no one can deny it. And then you'd think, whoever was guilty of this should be apologizing by now, and they're not. It could happen again tomorrow, and it's happened so many times already, resulting in death. It's beyond words. Although I think my half-sister needs to let go of the past, I have a lot of understanding for that. I know what it's like to have PTSD; being able to and wanting to are sometimes two completely different things.

Richard's head nurse was also the one who forced me to take him in, incomprehensibly corrupt. That way, they could be done with it and uphold their reputation, having helped another patient so well. Meanwhile, they knew everything about Richard's past, and I knew nothing. I only discovered that much later; they laughed about it. Richard was a very kind-hearted man, though he could sometimes make terrible mistakes when cornered. He, too, had a very troubled past.

Richard said she was buried on the Strabrechtse Heide. I don't believe that for a second. She may have been held captive in Dutroux's cellars after the kidnapping. Especially given the discovery of a pair of jeans there with their legs folded inwards, this could be considered a partially proven fact. Nobody wears pants like that. The parents didn't recognize the jeans as such because the knees were completely worn down, how sad. They did say that...

It could have been Tanja's trousers because of the inward-turning legs. Perhaps they couldn't and didn't want to face reality at that moment.

This is one possibility of what might have happened; she might still be alive. Richard often wore his shirts that way when I first met him, with the sleeves turned in, which was also very bizarre. Perhaps it was to remind the head nurse, Van den E, daily of what they had done.

I tried to get more information from Richard. His ex-in-laws knew Wim S., Richard told me one day during the confession, which lasted about three days.

Apparently, the contact between Richard and my family had already been established much earlier, something I hadn't known for a long time. I only discovered this after living with him for twenty years. He could remain silent as a tomb and, for good reason, had a top-secret clearance in the US Army. I learned a lot from him; he wanted to share everything he knew with me, including certain state secrets. He taught me to be silent, in moments when it's necessary, when silence demands it.

His former in-laws were related to the woman my grandfather, Jan Steenbakkers, went into business with after his wife, my grandmother, died. It's possible that both families knew each other back then, and perhaps even much longer; that's the most logical conclusion to be drawn from this story and the research into it. Grandfather had died suspiciously. Richard was a poor artist with a large family who was abused and oppressed; he couldn't handle money. However, he also had exceptionally good qualities, and he was exceptionally intelligent in certain areas. He was abused by many people; in reality, he had a very kind nature and a gentle disposition. They literally destroyed him, starting in his childhood. He may also have grown up with foster parents, which further complicates the story.

A man named Wim lived in the institution. I spoke to him regularly. He once clung to me when I visited Richard many years later, who had unfortunately ended up there again after becoming paralyzed. The man in question looks like Wim S. and has the same first name. It's an institution that sometimes, for various reasons, gives people a different identity; they even asked me about it once. Wim, the man from the institution, used to live on Groeneweg in Uden, where I also lived as a baby. He told me about a score to settle with my foster father because he had abused his wife; it nearly cost him his life, he said. I don't know if this is actually Wim S.; there are other people named Wim!

When I started living with Richard—in November 1997, to be precise—I happened to read the book "The Hidden History" by Donna Tart, a remarkable book and bestseller at the time; it bears similarities to the Tanja Groen case.

Health Education

Freedom is, above all, freedom from addiction. In this sense, the Bible teaches us how to achieve freedom and how to achieve optimal clarity of mind, allowing us to function well.

In our current times, temptations abound. People don't hesitate to sell unhealthy products; even governments participate, while people once thought they could trust them. Only a small portion of humanity seems to have realized that reality is often different. The safety net we once had is increasingly flawed and starting to resemble a leaky sieve. Therefore, we must be vigilant and trust God that if we do good, we will receive it. The reverse is also true, of course: good behavior is rewarded because God sees everything. Addictions can threaten our existence in many ways: financially, it can affect our health, or it can affect our position in society. Being addicted doesn't feel good, and that's perhaps the most important thing. Learn to listen to your body; it tells you exactly what you need. In that sense, addictions can be confusing and mask pain, although this is often temporary. Ultimately, you always return to the foundation, which should be good. Create structure in your life.

For years, I searched for a way to quit smoking. It felt impossible, but I found a method and supplemented it with a second, self-developed, step-by-step approach to overcoming addiction. This method is applicable to any addiction and costs nothing. In fact, most addictions ultimately cost a lot of money, so it's profitable. Moreover, it will make you a better person. You'll feel better, that's for sure, and much clearer. Addictions are confusing; being dependent on something is never pleasant. Whether it's smoking, food addiction, alcohol, drugs, gaming, you name it; you'll break free if you follow the program for a while. (This chapter also provides an overview of topics we studied during our Health Sciences studies.)

I'll briefly explain it here:

Breaking Habits

Being free from addictions is the path to happiness.

At some point in my life, I decided I'd had enough of addictions and was primarily looking for a way to quit smoking. It was a very bad habit that had slowly crept in and was also influenced by circumstances. For example, if your housemate smokes, quitting immediately becomes much more difficult, and it can be a partial reason why you still smoke.

Taking certain medications can have an effect; consuming certain stimulants: many people know that a cup of coffee can taste much better with a cigarette, and the same goes for alcohol. However, delicious doesn't always mean healthy; on the contrary.

Bible study helped me realize that I needed to improve my life, and eventually, I read the entire Bible from A to Z and understood it. Not everyone can say that.

That's how I discovered that the medication I was taking, due to the abuse and brain damage, might actually be doing more harm than good to my body. It was temporary circumstances that prompted the prescription. My physical condition at some point, something that can also improve, although Western medicine doesn't always mention this.

That's certainly how it felt. All cells in the body are constantly being renewed. Of course, this process slows down as we age, but I'm far from old. Brain and nerve cells are known to recover very slowly from damage, unlike most other cells that can reproduce very quickly. Healing is therefore often a natural process, and human intervention isn't always wise. Good nutrition, in particular, is literally vital.

And that was true. I certainly wouldn't be alive if I had continued taking those pills unnecessarily for years. It was a form of medication that can shorten your life by twenty to thirty years. Prescribed for a condition I didn't even have. Doctors often receive bonuses from the pharmaceutical industry for prescribing certain medications and making certain diagnoses. The diagnosis I wrongly received in the 1990s was a prime example and very popular at the time. Healthcare often revolves solely around money these days, so how can you ever get objective diagnoses? That's only possible if money plays no part, which it does.

It would be best to pay the doctor as long as the patient is healthy (or alive), and not the other way around, paying the doctor for treatment. In that case, money can be a perverse incentive to treat, something that, of course, must be avoided at all costs.

"Breaking Habits" is a program that breaks habits in general. You start with that, but you don't focus on the addiction itself. Focusing on it is also very counterproductive. The more you think about it, the harder it becomes to stay away from it. Whether it's smoking, drugs, or any other addiction, the trick is to not focus on it and find distraction. When you quit smoking, you often think of terrible withdrawal symptoms, which also apply to drugs. However, because you gradually reduce your intake with this method, you won't experience these symptoms; on the contrary, you'll feel better and better.

The first part of the program focuses on, as the name suggests: breaking habits.

If you break habits in general, letting go of the addiction will also become easier.

In this phase, you're more or less forced not to think about the addiction; letting go is crucial.

The program:

For three weeks, you'll do an exercise every day that helps you break habits. During this period, you'll choose something each day that you do differently than you're used to.

Suppose you drink a cup of coffee every morning after waking up, then for one day you don't drink coffee at that time, but something else, like tea.

The next day, you're allowed to go back to normal, and then you find something else to change, like not watching television for a day, or going to a different supermarket, cycling instead of driving, and so on.

It makes you aware; activities that always seemed so normal become a little less normal. It's the beginning of breaking habits. Try to maintain this for three weeks. You'll notice that you start to feel different, which will make it easier to break the habit that has become an addiction. You can then break it much more easily.

The second part of the program is an extension of the first:

Setting Boundaries

I'll explain this using my own situation. I forced myself to stop smoking during the day, and by five o'clock in the afternoon, I was allowed again, except for that one cigarette in the morning. I had switched to very light rolling tobacco much earlier, instead of cigarettes. It all helps reduce the nicotine receptors in your body.

It was difficult at first, but the thought that I'd be back at five o'clock always reassured me. I looked for all sorts of things to distract myself from thinking about smoking: going outside, walking, cycling, or whatever.

As you smoke less, the nicotine receptors in your body decrease and you feel less of a need to smoke. This applies to any addiction, although it works differently in the body, and with drugs, for example, you have different receptors. Your bodies urge to seek satisfaction or satiety through gaming, food, sex, whatever it may be, is often unhealthy behavior focused on lust. Abstinence is healthier; in that sense, we can take a cue from monks and nuns; they often live to be very old. I found it increasingly easier to not smoke. Sometimes I'd forget it was five o'clock in the afternoon and that I was allowed to smoke again. I stuck to this rule because I was very motivated to quit. Gradually, I started feeling better and better. It had a positive effect in many ways.

I still stick to it and hardly smoke anymore. I might even smoke that occasional roll-up because you need nicotinic acid in your body. Often, not everything is bad unless you've crossed a certain threshold.

Healthcare has become an out-of-control institution that started very small centuries ago and has become a Titanic doomed to sink. In many countries, an average of half the government budget goes to healthcare, including direct and indirect costs. For many people and companies, it's a source of income or a way to make money. It has become a multi-billion dollar business with a huge amount of money at stake, the stakes are high, and the patient often no longer comes first—which is truly an understatement.

Financial interests, in particular, weigh heavily. The patient's interests have become increasingly irrelevant, making objective diagnoses increasingly difficult. Budgets within healthcare institutions must be balanced. Especially since privatization, things have gotten completely out of control.

Alternative and natural medicine is being increasingly suppressed, including through internet censorship. Everything must be chemically controlled according to WEF and WHO standards. How awful! Where once the witch doctor knew everything about medicinal herbs and all sorts of methods to promote human health, it is now the pharmaceutical industry that, through laws and regulations, is able to force people into all sorts of treatments that are not always desirable or sensible. A middle ground is, at the very least, important.

This is an undesirable situation that the average citizen is barely aware of due to a lack of medical knowledge, but also due to the trust they have always had in healthcare, and doctors in particular.

Defense

When my husband died, he told me a lot in the last days of his life that I didn't know, especially about my family. He'd known them much longer than I'd known him; I didn't even know that.

It turns out my father was my foster father. Both parents were probably foster parents. I have no reason to doubt Richard's stories, and it got much worse. He even asked him to kill me. I see my foster father as the perpetrator. My foster mother had a good character, but she was also severely abused by him.

Abuse runs like a thread through my foster father's life. He was guilty of it many times. I suspect him of many criminal offenses. One of them, at least, is that, for no apparent reason, at the end of my studies, he wrestled me to the ground, stamped on my back, and kicked me in the head. Just like that, out of nowhere. I was so shocked that I couldn't react to defend myself. It had a huge impact on my life; something snapped after everything I'd been through with him. Perhaps even literally, brain damage, and I had trouble with my left ear, near my temple, where he kicked with those clumsy paws. That's something I've always had trouble with. So his intention was to kick me to death; the distance from your ear to your temple is about five centimeters, and he kicked very hard. I couldn't report it, not even when some time later, or perhaps a while before, my half-sister threw a heavy tin ashtray at my head from less than a meter away. I managed to dodge it, but I'd had enough. I called the police, and they came knocking shortly after, telling me to go to social services. I did, and it solved nothing. I was always blamed; they were never included in the story, not even their jealousy and aggression. I received the ashtray when my foster parents moved. It's still somewhere in the garage with a big dent in it, caused by the loud bang against the wall back then.

He's a terrible man, impossible to reason with, and he completely turned my half-sister against me; she's even worse.

Probably because of my biological father's inheritance, of which I never saw a penny or a dime. I've found a lot of evidence for this, including that he must have left a lot, and that at least a significant portion of what I was entitled to was kept from me because I saw nothing of it, for the simple reason that I wasn't allowed to know anything about it.

The notary in Heesch should have asked me if I wanted the villa where Jan lived until he died. I didn't get time to think about it. They ask at an inconvenient time for you. Again, I was surprised. I knew nothing about it, and then suddenly I'm offered a villa. After about a minute, the response was: "Oh, you don't want that, then no!" That was it. I had just graduated and was still thinking about a great career, something I'd worked so hard for my whole life. I didn't immediately envision that in Heesch, but they didn't tell me anything else, and I didn't have time to think about it, but I hadn't denied it either. They reached their own conclusion based on a decision they'd made ages ago: that I would get that villa didn't fit their vision in any way. It was before they published the book about me; I still had some friends where I lived, and all their slander and libel hadn't yet lost them.

That's why my foster father wanted to kill me; he's been abusing me since I was a child. I never really understood it until Richard told me a lot about it a few years ago.

The other inheritance issue concerns compensation for someone who took Risperdal. Due to lies from family, I was misdiagnosed and wrongly forced to take Risperdal for years. They went so far, especially my half-sister and my foster father that they had a book written about me, full of lies and deceit, based on stolen medical records and a diary my foster father kept about me, which was quite sick in itself. This book is called "Everything is Carmen" (Everything is Carmen), and its libel and slander. I tried to have it withdrawn from print, but I couldn't. It's even available for loan from the public library; half of Gemert has read it. It's truly awful how, out of jealousy and for money, they even threw my medical records out there, and it's not even true; it's all gossip, lies, and slander. My life was ruined by them. I couldn't have a career, and everything I tried to build with Richard was destroyed just as brutally by them. It's beyond words. Those were their activities. My foster father, after retiring, had a full-time job doing it behind my back, and for my half-sister, it was even a government-subsidized art project. I felt terrible for Richard.

They probably commissioned the author, Alma Mathijssen, to write the book because of compensation; someone from Canada received a whopping eight billion. That's enough to start a serious war. My half-sister's "friends" are mainly from Romania and Ukraine; she's a member of the Russian Orthodox Church. Well, friends! Are you a friend if you stand at someone's window at night to harass an innocent person? A friend is honest and should know better. People without a place to stay who deliver the homeless newspaper quickly become your friend, especially if you take them in and offer them shelter. She gets up to all sorts of ridiculous things like this, and that's by no means all.

My cousin called me around the time it happened, about the book and the compensation. He told me I supposedly had a brother, but he didn't elaborate. In hindsight, I came to understand. His behavior revealed he suddenly had considerable money at his disposal. I wasn't informed of this either, and I haven't seen a cent of it.

My half-sister bothers me a lot and I've come to see her as my foster father's hitman. This also aligns with the stories Richard told me. Neighbors have caused Richard and me an excessive amount of trouble. We've experienced the craziest things, and I didn't quite understand the reasons for it when it happened. In retrospect, I suspect she was behind it all, constantly bothering us. She has a bad character, even though she can put on such a good front. She's mentally disabled, possibly with acquired brain injury. They had my car vandalized, and she desecrated my husband's grave. They tried to kick down my door, broke into my house, and stole my belongings. The car was a very nice Volvo, which I had to get rid of because of the extent of the damage.

One evening, a neighbor—luckily, he no longer lives next door—even came and hacked at our front door with an axe.

This is just a small sample of the many criminal acts she committed against me. Richard couldn't survive this. Neither could my mother; she stood by me and was severely abused by both my foster father and half-sister.

And now I'm at the top of the list, says my foster father. That doesn't bode well. He never did much for me except obstruct me. I never received any gifts, unlike my half-sister, to whom hundreds of thousands of euros went.

Through corruption via the housing association, or rather a company they hired to replace cylinders at my request, they managed to get the key to my house. Often, when I had an appointment, I noticed someone had been in my house.

I tried to report several incidents, but often this wasn't possible. In some cases, the police sent someone from outreach services that did little else. I've heard they also bribed the police.

To stop them, I started writing this book. People have often become very volatile and draw conclusions based on half the story, often hearsay. About issues that could be disastrous for the person in question, could destroy someone's life. People from whom you should expect more, for example, because they are highly educated and hold a responsible position. My foster sister is one such person. In forty years, she never gave me a single chance to have a decent conversation. I saw her at most at birthday parties, which I hardly ever attended anyway, because the presence of my half-sister always managed to throw a wrench in the works for me, often in a serious way. Sometimes I saw my foster sister once every two years for fifteen minutes. I was not allowed any contact with her children at all, for which I don't know the reason either. She thought she knew everything about me and acted as a kind of mediator, one who wanted to destroy me even further. She abused her power in a horrific way. While she owed her doctorate to me for her accelerated Nursing Science degree, she took practically everything from me under duress from her ex-boyfriend. I had just about managed to tell her that he was gay. Only after forty years did it finally sink in. Fine, but don't pretend! Fooling your wife, secretly cheating, stealing from your in-laws and smearing them. In that respect, I'm glad he came out, although as far as I'm concerned, his new partner shouldn't have been present at my foster mother's funeral. Shocking!

I'll just be honest. I haven't been given this opportunity before, and it's my last cry for help to stop these people and restore my name. I haven't done anything wrong, the government at least agrees on that.

A few weeks ago, they were in my house again; this has to stop. For years, I've tried to work things out through conversations. I've learned a lot, but talking it out is impossible; it's impossible to communicate with them. Their behavior is often indecent and antisocial.

How they treated my foster mother deeply affected me. I wanted to care for her every day, but was literally kicked out time and again by either my foster father or my half-sister.

It's all too horrific, and they just keep going. I've broken off contact; it was unbearable.

My parents were married in community of property; I haven't seen a will, even though they had one drawn up together. I've been kept out of everything and know nothing. They tell me nothing, even though I have the same rights as my two sisters. Richard can claim they're not my biological parents, but they've never told me directly. It's just a suspicion; on paper, they're simply my parents. I have no further correspondence. I threw away all the horrible messages I received from them and the powdered letters as quickly as possible, although there must still be some remnants of those letters in a corner of the garage. It was all too horrific. Born with a helmet on, it can work out well, but the sensitivities that such people often have can also be used in the wrong way.

Nostradamus

anja Groen wanted to study Health Sciences, a holistic program that no longer fits at all with the general trend of globalization. Those in power at major international organizations like the WEF and the WHO have very different plans; they don't want to know much about the natural healing that the program was partly based on. In fact, it often involves information they prefer to keep from people; there's not enough money to be made from it, and the pharmaceutical industry wants to maintain its power.

Health education was one of these seven specializations in the Health Sciences program and a key component of the path to natural healing. The specialization I took was a kind of medical program without medication, primarily focused on exercise, Movement Sciences. These kinds of time-consuming and more natural treatments are increasingly fading into the background. People no longer want anything natural; it must be primarily chemical and profitable.

Consider, for example, the tropical rainforests, the enormous wealth of medicinal plants, and the way all of this was rapidly destroyed. It will take centuries for this to ever return. If it ever returns, the earth has already been derailed. It's called the old world, plants and fruits of the old world. To this day, however, the new world is focused on destruction. Let's try to save everything that's left of the old. People who adhere to the new world have largely lost their minds, and at least their connection to the earth, through perversity or adherence to the devil.

Nostradamus, already one of the leading advocates of many more natural healing methods in the sixteenth century, was persecuted in his time, particularly by the Church Inquisition. That's why he passed on all his findings in secret messages, hidden in verses called quatrains. Ultimately, his family had to flee France.

Because of the danger of persecution—the Church Inquisition was unrelenting at the time—they fled and ended up near Oss. I'm in touch with one of their descendants; they were true natural healers. It wasn't far from this area that Vincent van Gogh created some of his finest works, sometime earlier, just before the Industrial Revolution.

At that time, there was even a small train running from Wesel and Goch in Germany to the area we're discussing now: Uden, Veghel, and Schijndel. Surnames were often spelled in different ways back then, and while there were all sorts of municipal registers, the strict documentation of absolutely everything, as we know it today, was, of course, nonexistent. So, Goch could very easily be a corruption of van Gogh, or vice versa.

It's probably not purely coincidental that when Vincent van Gogh finally left for France, he ended up in Saint-Rémy-de-Provence, the town near Arles where Nostradamus was born and where he even worked in the clinic where Vincent was temporarily hospitalized, although it wasn't yet a psychiatric hospital. Nostradamus pursued a medical doctorate in Montpellier, which is also the city where this friend's ancestors came from. They adopted a different name in the Netherlands and settled not far from Oss in a small hamlet. The neighborhood in Uden where I lived for a while also had the same name as that hamlet; the house was located on Groeneweg.

Nostradamus predicted that the entire region, where I returned to live after my studies, would one day become a very prosperous area. It's starting to look that way, not least because of ASML, the international chip manufacturer, and also because of Gemert-Eindhoven Castle.

The village where I live is an herb village—everyone calls it a village—but it has city rights and was once a principality, an independent city-state annexed by the Kingdom of the Netherlands over two centuries ago.

Not only that, but there used to be a seminary, the Major Seminary, housed in the immense castle in the center of the village, and the "village" had a Latin school.

Someone from Gemert founded Maastricht University. Moreover, Gemert was one of the most important bailiwicks of the Teutonic Order in Europe, a society of clergymen who wielded considerable power for centuries. Until around the beginning of the twentieth century, one of the main locations was Gemert Castle. After that, it came into the hands of the Spiritans, the Congregation of the Holy Spirit, a Catholic order.

Not long ago, the monks, who had been housed there for about a century, sold it. A luxury Hilton hotel, the Hilton Curio, will be located there. Moreover, the gatehouse now houses a fantastic restaurant. A chef who literally cooked up (Michelin) stars in Nuenen has moved his business to Gemert to take on a new challenge. Preparations are in full swing.

Van der G

S o, they had taken over my foster sister, her ex's family, and they also fought for the grandchildren's attention. I won't go into that in detail here for privacy reasons. They simply took my foster sister away from us; there was no party for them to celebrate their union, all together for forty years. They did, however, once spend a night in a bridal suite to fake a wedding night; everything was fake with them. Except for the children, who were all he cared about, very sweet children indeed. It's a shame I was never able to connect with them.

Sometimes I would take him food when he was sick; things calmed down quickly afterward, although he initially even pointed a camera at my house.

One day, he gave me flowers. I could no longer do anything wrong, but ten years later it was too late. He died from a life of crime, alcohol, and drugs. They always managed to find him, which meant he kept pushing the boundaries. Yet another neighbor who seemed to have been planted here to make life as uncomfortable as possible for Richard and me, or rather, miserable, by family members who had contacts with the housing association and even managed to get a key to my house that way.

Someone from my foster sister and her partner's circle, completely out of the blue, once told me at a birthday party where I was barely able to attend that they were in touch with him and might send him to me. I was stunned and didn't know why. Because I believed that even a gay man should be straight in some respect, and that infidelity was reprehensible. That must have been the reason; healthy discussions were impossible; I had some really good reasons for my thinking. It was understandable that he didn't want to share his infidelity with the rest of the world; only his friends were supposed to know. What a theatrical performance he put on every time. My foster parents, unaware of any wrongdoing in that regard, were too old-fashioned to fully grasp how utterly and utterly they were being fooled. They wouldn't accept it from me, probably afraid of losing contact with the grandchildren, who were being used as playthings—blackmail, really.

Pointing a camera at someone's house is absolutely forbidden, of course. He did what God and everyone else had forbidden; that was his trademark, and he took immense pride in always doing everything differently. Provocation was truly his thing. They did everything differently; they wanted to reinvent the wheel. They also handled intimacy differently, which, in their case, is a very polite expression for the vile way in which they abused absolutely everything and everyone.

This, too, had serious consequences. Someone entered my house without my permission at least ten times—a burglary, as it's called. I couldn't report it; the same woman from the council would always come to the door, and that incident, too, would quickly be covered up, all orchestrated by the three survivors in collaboration with authorities, or what's left of my foster family, because they're fighting it out. Imagine, I never did anything wrong. This all happened out of jealousy. The way institutions allowed themselves to be manipulated was extremely dangerous. We think we're safe in this modern world of democracy, but the reality is completely different.

They even managed to plant listening devices, and if I said anything about it, they said I was seeing ghosts and was confused, giving them another good reason to pillory me before the authorities. Meanwhile, everything I discovered was true, and there was much more. Certainly, I'm highly gifted and, as such, have a very strong sixth sense, something they've long denied.

They managed to instill in me by falsely stuffing me with pills and calling me crazy. How awful! I have a medical degree that's higher than a basic medical degree, and their diplomas, even taken together, are a stark contrast. I had to work incredibly hard to achieve all this; they ruined everything, all my chances, and more. One day, a doctor even showed up unannounced at my door to perform euthanasia on me, all orchestrated by the aforementioned trio. It was a real shock, I can assure you. Even I, after everything I've been through, even then, felt like a complete low point. These are traumatic experiences. You feel powerless; the ground is slipping away from under your feet. It's all so unlawful and government-driven. And that man smelled, literally—who does something like that? He went to the bathroom. I've never smelled such a foul, strong, sickly odor of urine. Ugh, this was literally and figuratively a very mean, dirty trick.

My foster sister once mentioned the name of the neighbor who had moved in right behind me, trying to warn me, which came as a complete shock, both the warning and the name she mentioned. I was completely unaware of any wrongdoing; it was a complete distortion of the facts that she also wanted revenge. I haven't had a chance to speak to her in forty years and saw her at most once a year at family events, and even then usually for no more than fifteen minutes. While she's always talking about me and really only talks about me, even when I'm practically standing there, it's all become so crude that I'm constantly amazed. She owes her doctorate to me; without me, she would never have ended up in Maastricht, nor would she have been able to build a career even if she had only pursued a shortened two-year doctorate in a much less demanding field. So serious, that neighbor behind us was one of the worst criminals in half the Netherlands. We were really not happy when he moved in behind us. After everything we'd already been through, that was truly the last straw. He was a terrifying guy; he made the whole village unsafe with his pit bull, which he usually let loose when he was out and about in his wooden clogs with one or more of his buddies. Only, you hardly ever saw him.

I'll never forget the moment he moved in behind me. Of all people, he was the one. It couldn't have been worse, that's how it felt at that moment.

Especially after everything they'd already hunted down, our neighborhood seemed to have become a place where the most impossible people were stuck, which hadn't always been a pleasant and peaceful place to live.

He wasn't the only one. Even Van der G. spent some time here, immediately after his release. He was the one who spent years in prison for the murder of a Dutch politician. The reason he ended up practically around the corner from me should be obvious: through connections, staying at a house belonging to a friend of my foster sister's partner.

I still remember the moment he was released; it was as if people in the neighborhood knew, or at least sensed it. I was stressed at that moment, because of the enormous task of caring for my husband, who was seriously ill at the time, all by myself. Because of that...

I had too much adrenaline in my blood, and I had to run all day to get everything done, for years. A period that, thankfully, is now long behind me.

Partly due to the stress, I often nearly collapsed, and at that moment, quite literally, in the playground near the house where Van der G had settled.

Some people came running towards me; there were an abnormal number of people around at that moment, as if everyone sensed something was wrong, and it wasn't just my fall. People even sat down on the ground; it seemed like a kind of greeting to a man, at least unknown to me. That's Gemert, formerly a Free Lordship. Everyone was welcome, and there were few laws. Out of fear, people were overly friendly, also because they knew there was no other way. You wanted to protect yourself a little. Danger was everywhere, and you were fair game. No one would come to help you if something serious happened. This is a conclusion that can be drawn from the above events. For some people, it was precisely the reason to come live here; the lawlessness allowed them to go about their business without reprisals.

From the window, I saw him walking, suddenly a free man, and the murderer who had been the subject of so much commotion. Everyone, of course, had wondered if he could just move back to the town where he had a house, immediately after his release. Not so. As a way station, he too ended up in Gemert. We're kind of used to it, though you never really get used to it. It's like hate; you never get used to that either.

When I attended a meeting of the political movement I'm affiliated with a few days later, I wasn't exactly thrilled to see him there. Is he already making a mistake, I wondered! Luckily, there were security measures, and my eyes have a certain magic; I, too, can intimidate if necessary. He slunk off, his tail between his legs, even though he was standing less than two meters away, staring at me with a horrific look in his eyes. What a scary guy. The meeting was at the Cacaofabriek, a cultural institution in Helmond.

When I happened to see my foster sister at my foster parents' house one day, I told her something about the meeting. She reacted very strangely and suddenly started talking about her son's boyfriend, that he had a girlfriend. What a back street, I thought to myself. Remarkable.

What seemed even more remarkable was her request some time later to go to the movies at the Cacaofabriek. I shuddered; it's a remote spot on the edge of town with a huge parking lot, pitch black in the evenings and at night. How can your little sister, whom you've always protected—something that's also deeply ingrained—change so much? My system still can't handle this. I'm acting in good faith, a form of projection to avoid assuming someone might have bad intentions, even though I often sense it very quickly. I give people a fair chance, time and time again, and I'm not likely to close the door for good. You'd have to have really messed things up, and they did.

That question was very suspicious; no one would have thought of it, especially not if you live in a city with the best cinemas, like in her case. Knowing, too, that the public transport connection to Eindhoven—in my case, still without a car at that point—was much better than to Helmond.

No one from Gemert goes to the movies in Helmond. It's all very suspicious, if you ask me.

You don't need to ask the other Gemert residents, by the way; they're usually as silent as a tomb; no one wants trouble or to get involved. A few people do spill the beans, and then you usually know enough.

Familiar territory, at least for Van der G, the Cacaofabriek.

I expected more integrity from my foster sister, a long-time manager of a very large healthcare institution; although this also fit seamlessly into the list of things she'd already dropped in my direction, and not just dropped, how false. I didn't recognize anything in her anymore of the cheerful, sweet girl she used to be. In turn, she was completely destroyed by her in-laws. Fortunately, that didn't happen to me. My in-laws were so kind and sweet that my husband's ex kept visiting my mother-in-law in the United States, even crawling into bed with her, even with her new husband, and still calling her "mother." Looking for, or perhaps searching, looking for, money. Everyone says you can't rely on your in-laws for anything. I was grateful to Mom and owe her many good things, especially Bible study and the strong faith she instilled in me. RIP Mary Lee Barton. She lived to a very old age, almost a hundred, and I still miss her.

Part II
Yellow

Nune Ville

une Ville is the building located next to the original parsonage of the Reformed Church in Nuenen. The building was occupied for a long time by the Begemann family. The building next door, the parsonage, was occupied for a time by the Van Gogh family. The gardens are also adjacent and have been largely preserved in their original state.

Nune Ville can be visited on Saturdays and is located opposite the Van Gogh Village Museum in Nuenen, although there is little real collaboration.

Vincent van Gogh's father was a minister in Nuenen for a time during the first half of the 1880s. Vincent also lived in Nuenen for two years, officially with his parents, directly across from the museum.

It was no easy task for either party. Vincent left home at a young age and was accustomed to freedom; returning to his parents' house was not easy, and that proved to be the case. He soon sought refuge elsewhere in the village and was given shelter by the sexton of the Catholic Church. Nuenen is situated on the edge of the monastic belt, one of the most Catholic parts of Europe, an area of approximately fifty square kilometers with numerous monasteries, most of which have been repurposed in recent years due to a decline in the church or even literally demolished. The office of clergyman, brother, or sister no longer really captures the imagination in the Netherlands.

There used to be all sorts of reasons for someone to join a particular order. Due to the relaxation of values and norms, there are also fewer reasons for joining, such as illegitimate children who were hidden away in monasteries as they grew to adulthood. Monasteries have lost popularity, not least because of all the abuse scandals. Moreover, to join, you have to bring money; if you don't have it, it becomes very difficult. Joining an order is less easy than many people think.

Celibacy certainly played a role in the decline of monastic life, especially in today's society where lust has become an increasingly important factor, celibacy seems completely passé. Although you could also wonder how passé it actually is to just jump into a suitcase with anyone. People consider it normal to have extramarital affairs—at least in the Netherlands, where people genuinely believe anything goes—but firstly; they don't realize the potential consequences. The pharmaceutical industry profits from it. Secondly, there's little awareness of the pain people inflict on each other by being married and giving their love to another. In the Netherlands, it's considered perfectly normal, and you're practically labeled Jehovah's Witness if you adhere to the biblical doctrine of fidelity, at least in the Catholic South.

Contrary to what the Vatican prescribed for centuries, we should study the Bible. I would also recommend making less distinction between Christian churches. They are about the same God and Christ; one isn't always better than the other; cooperation is important.

We're doing well if we follow the Bible. It never says, for example, that a priest shouldn't marry. The Old Testament literally states that a priest may marry, but only a virgin, which seems very logical in this context. It could have prevented a lot of problems in the past.

Nuenen had a Protestant enclave, created by industrialization when people moved from the western Netherlands, which was much more Calvinist at the time, to southern regions to establish businesses such as the textile industry.

Incidentally, the diocese of 's-Hertogenbosch had for centuries been open to discussions about faith between Protestants, who adhere more closely to the faith as described in the Bible, and Catholics, from whom the Bible had long been kept away. The Brotherhood of Our Lady was a good example of how they sought to initiate dialogue. It is beyond doubt that cooperation and a pooling of resources were necessary.

Vincent's father forbade him from contact with Catholic farmers—at that time, the countryside was predominantly agricultural—which was not easy for Vincent; he wanted to be able to connect with everyone.

This was certainly also important for his profession as a painter; he enjoyed painting the people around him and was fascinated by farming life in Southeast Brabant. During this time, he particularly enjoyed drawing farm life and frequently sought models. Think of farmers plowing and women working in the fields. There are countless examples of his work from that period, primarily depicting farm life. The home weaving workshops that arose with the advent of the textile industry were also a favorite subject for Vincent. While Reverend Van Gogh specifically did not want Vincent to have contact with people from these social classes, this often clashed with his father.

This was one of the reasons Vincent connected with Pieter Kruijsen, a pharmacist working at Huize Padua, the institution located near Nuenen where artists often sought refuge throughout history. For privacy reasons, it has been kept completely off the books, as Huize Padua was long a psychiatric institution, founded by priests who had opened the gates of the centuries-old buildings to help their fellow human beings.

Pieter Kruijsen lived in nearby Erp and, during the period he was in contact with Vincent, set up the institution's painting department. Pieter's daughter was in touch with Vincent's youngest sister, proving that there was indeed a connection between the two families.

Erp was relatively easy to reach from Nuenen. You could take the train to Helmond from Eeneind station in Nuenen and then the tram to Erp, where there was a tram station. Gemert, too, was on the route and a place where many artists gathered, particularly at Tramstation De Keizer, an establishment that still exists. Eeneind station has been closed, and the tram line no longer exists. Only a tourist tram line serves to evoke the atmosphere of yesteryear around Gemert, where a unique museum commemorating that time has been established: the Boerenbondsmuseum (Farmers' Union Museum). Those who go there can see what life was like in Vincent's time: farm life, including agriculture as it was practiced at that time; a small school dating from the last century or earlier; and the first bank in the region, the Boerenleenbank (Farmers' Loan Bank). It's truly remarkable to see how everything has been brought back to the past: an old blacksmith's shop; Weaving mill, café. You name it, it's all there to see, and the surroundings are even more impressive; nature hasn't changed much over the centuries. Including pollard willows, poplars, and even plowing farmers, if you're lucky. Well worth a visit.

The Gemert landscape is strongly reminiscent of the many sketches, paintings, and drawings Vincent made during that time. Gemert is and was a beautiful village and part of the original landscape.

Much has been preserved. It was once a principality and, as such, very large in area. A huge and imposing medieval castle stands in the center of Gemert.

In the first edition of the letters, written by Vincent van Gogh to his brother Theo and published by his sister-in-law Jo van Gogh-Bongers, Theo's wife, it is stated that letters that were too personal, medically sensitive, and problematic were omitted. The letters form the basis of almost all books written about Vincent van Gogh, so censorship began in the early twentieth century when the letters were published, and much more was censored later.

Consequently, the entire episode about Huize Padua is largely unknown, even though there are still people in Gemert and its immediate surroundings who can tell stories about the time Vincent spent hanging out and painting there; he even had a nickname there.

Therefore, some of the history should actually be rewritten. A painful history, that's clear, yet this involves major interests and Dutch government funding, not just the family's, although it's understandable that you'd rather not have a family member's life story in the books. While this is understandable, fame has a downside. Privacy concerns don't allow you to simply manipulate reality; the complete story must be told. People have a right to that. In the case of Vincent van Gogh paintings, there are many stakeholders, not just the family who profited and could afford a grand villa in Wassenaar after selling the entire collection to the state. Everyone wants to live there, in the dunes on one of the Netherlands' most beautiful beaches. I wish them well; that's not the point. However, it would be nice if they would also grant someone else something, even though, as a family, they have stipulated a kind of veto power in matters related to this. There are no legal rules for this; it's a bit of a guessing game. After serving as a parsonage for a time in the first half of the twentieth century, Nune Ville was purchased by the Van Gogh family. More than fifty years later, it came into the hands of a Nuenen housing association and is currently privately occupied, housing a kind of museum. Visitors can also experience the house and feel transported back in time. The Begemann sisters' rooms have been partially preserved, retaining their original atmosphere. There's even a secret room in the attic where a Jewish refugee hid during World War II—a truly impressive sight.

This building also has historical significance due to the fact that one of the daughters of the original owner, Reverend Begemann, had an affair with Vincent van Gogh.

Remarkably, Margot Begemann, the person in question, grew up in the house where Vincent had moved in with his parents. The family first lived in the house where the Van Gogh family eventually settled and then moved to Nune Ville, the house in question. About six months after moving in with his parents, Margot Begemann and Vincent van Gogh began a relationship. The gardens of both magnificent mansions have also been largely preserved in their original state and are directly adjacent.

The size of the gardens is striking; you don't often see them these days; they exude the atmosphere of yesteryear. The garden of Nune Ville is particularly striking, as not only the house but also the garden has been completely restored to its former glory. This property is open to the public.

Unlike the rectory where Vincent lived, although the original studio is still open on the first Saturday of the month, a visit can be combined with a visit to Nune Ville, which is open for tours every Saturday.

I thought it would be a nice idea to go there again, though also painful. It was the last museum visit I was able to make with Richard, my late husband, before he ultimately became very ill and died.

My last visit to Nune Ville also had disastrous consequences.

It seemed as if history was repeating itself.

At the time, Vincent was deemed unwell by the Begemann sisters, which resulted in Margot attempting suicide. Vincent's grief was immense. Although he had narrowly saved her life, she was left with permanent damage and had to spend the rest of her life in a hospital.

It didn't come to that in my case, and it never would, but I was also shown the door.

At that moment, I realized how Vincent must have felt when Margot's sisters told him he wasn't good enough. In that respect, it was a characterful museum visit, a step back in time, so to speak, albeit not in the most pleasant way.

Because of the extensive damage to my car, I sold it and cycled to Nuenen. The weather was glorious, though it was quite a long bike ride. Eeneind station no longer exists; Nuenen is accessible by bus from Gemert. The tourist tram line, also known locally as the silent killer because of its danger, only runs through Gemert. This nickname, incidentally, referred to the old tram from the past, although I still tremble a little when I see the newer one.

In that sense, Gemert has become even more isolated, this has not only disadvantages but also advantages. To get anywhere, you need a car. There's a bus to Eindhoven, the most common route to get anywhere, but getting there takes an hour, which is enough to get you out of the mood. First, you walk to the bus stop, wait for the bus; take a seat when it finally arrives, and then just hope for the best. I've witnessed all sorts of things happening several times, including collisions, but usually, nothing too serious.

You used to be able to take the tram to Veghel, and from there, there was even a train to Wezel, Germany. During the war, it was all destroyed by the Germans.

Full of enthusiasm, I arrived in Nuenen by bike, feeling quite sore, and walked into the beautiful Van Gogh Village Museum, located opposite Nune Ville. Pretty soon, I ended up in the cinema to watch a film about Vincent van Gogh's life in Brabant.

I found the film impressive and wanted to go outside for some fresh air. However, in the foyer, a museum employee approached me and I struck up a conversation. We talked about my first book; God is in Control, and its contents. She told me she'd like to read it.

They wanted to include it in their bookstore collection, partly because it's in English.

What great news! I wanted to tell my team leader right away, which is very difficult without a phone. For safety reasons, I can't take one with me on the road or when traveling. I walked to Albert Heijn to buy a notepad and some pencils after visiting the Van Gogh Church and several other interesting sights related to Vincent's life.

I'd had an important question about one of them for a while: there are two Clement's Churches in Nuenen, one in Nuenen and the other in nearby Gerwen. Nuenen claims that Vincent lived for a while in the parsonage next to their Clement's Church. However, the parsonage next to the Clement's Church looks much more like the one in Gerwen when you compare it to the surviving images from that period. This is also described in the letters as such.

Very bizarre, you'd almost think reality was manipulated to reinforce the story. This fits well with the image the people of Eindhoven paint, for example, with the expression "Nuenen dwars" (Nuenen cross). It's a closed community; all that glitters seems gold.

Finding the truth is important; it involves major interests, and in the case of the Van Gogh Museum in Amsterdam, it's about creating public money. The Van Gogh Museum Village staff member told me that they've started operating independently of Amsterdam, which is telling.

I sat down in the park and looked at the Potato Eaters statue. My walk outside at that moment, completely alone, was mainly about killing time. I decided that I still had the whole winter ahead of me to visit the museum more often, and that I wanted to go to Nune Ville, the house where Margot Begemann lived at the time. I'd heard so many stories about it and that afternoon I signed up for a tour at the little table in front of her house. When I arrived, I asked her about the two churches with the same name. This not only broke the ice, but it literally ignited her fire right before my eyes. I'm still astonished, almost a year later. This wasn't what I expected; I'd expected a slightly warmer welcome.

The first round was fully booked, and I had to wait over an hour.

Full of good cheer, I finally rang the doorbell. She opened the door and immediately told me I wasn't welcome, which I found quite shocking in the middle of the street, and I wondered why. She agreed when I told her how long I'd been waiting.

She made me wait again, but did come with a tea towel to dry the bench in front of her house so I could sit there. It had been raining that morning.

Finally, inside, she offered her condolences on the passing of my husband. She started firing all sorts of questions at me, about everything and nothing, accusing me of jumping from topic to topic, even though I was only answering the wide range of questions she posed.

She said I was mentally disturbed and asked me to leave again.

It reminded me of someone.

I graduated from high school and then got a doctorate in a fairly demanding medical field, and that wasn't all.

I found everything she said very shocking, and she was very aggressive. I was literally thrown out after a while.

I'm anything but a liar, and I'm someone who thoroughly investigates things before coming out.

She asked a lot of questions and concluded that everything I said was a lie. How shocking!

She asked me to leave again.

I refused to drink the dirty, sticky glass of water she'd given me, left the building, got my bike, and went home.

I was completely shocked, actually; this was so insulting.

I've been doing so much research for years and don't lie. On the way home, I wasn't feeling well, stopped at a restaurant for a drink, and ordered cold (chocolate) milk.

This is an example of what can happen when people spread gossip; stories take on a life of their own. The most important part of all the gossip about me has never been verified with me and is based on lies and deceit, out of jealousy, for possessions and money. People who commit libel and slander in this way are completely unable to communicate. I did everything I could to have their book about me, "Alles is Carmen," withdrawn from print. I reported it to the authorities and investigated who the perpetrator was. My suspicions were confirmed. Even the Dutch publisher refused my request. What they did was character assassination.

If an artist did sell anything, in Vincent's time, there was usually little written down. Paris was a popular city for artists at the time; competition was fierce, but people still sought each other out. Many collections were lost during World War II; the war was largely about art.

The European aristocracy consisted largely of Jews. Many of them ended up in Auschwitz with a suitcase containing their last possessions. They were forced onto freight trains from all over Europe, all the way to Greece.

These were heavy suitcases, also filled with gold—no other reason. The story about the gold fillings is hardly credible. Hitler needed considerably more money to pay for the transports, which wasn't initially a direct concern of the German government. Although it was a less comfortable journey, crammed into a square meter with ten people for three days, people still assumed at that time that everything would turn out fine.

Upon arrival in Auschwitz, the Jews were given a shower, they were told, before a barber was given a minute to cut their hair, all supposedly for disinfection. The supposed shower was actually the gas chamber, but most of them didn't live to tell the tale. The romanticized images of labor camps, as we know them from films, tell only a small part of the story. Most people didn't end up in a labor camp, although those from the camps often ultimately met their deaths. When the train entered the camp, it usually went straight to the Disaster, as the area with the underground gas chambers was called.

It's now been eighty years since this war ended, thanks to the efforts of Americans, British, Russians, and Canadians. A large part of my family, most of them Meijer, can't live to tell the tale.

At least they ended up there. When the train passed through the familiar wrought-iron gate with the inscription "Arbeit macht frei," freedom wasn't exactly what beckoned. The contrast couldn't be greater. As soon as people were finally released from that train, most immediately dove into the bushes and dropped dead on the spot; when someone dies, their bowels also empty. If they could still speak, the only thing they could manage was: "Thirst!"

It's criminal; nothing worse has ever happened than the Holocaust. Not to mention the suffering of Christ, which, however, only affected one person, though no less terrible for that. It's terrible; terrible events are still happening everywhere, which is why every form of aggression must stop; weapons should be absolutely forbidden. Diplomacy offers many more solutions. The stories that Germans extracted the gold from dental fillings are completely absurd; it really came from somewhere else, from suitcases, and some of it is probably still hidden somewhere in the Philippines. They lied to each other about everything.

Hitler and his comrade Göring, though separately, both wanted to start a museum of modern art and each stole approximately several million works of art in Europe, primarily in France and the Netherlands, primarily from Jews. The paintings were stored in underground tunnels.

After the war, these works ended up everywhere. And of course, works by Vincent van Gogh could have been among them; that seems more logical than questionable. After the publication of the books containing his letters to Theo, Vincent began to gain a reputation posthumously. A few years later, at the beginning of the twentieth century, ten thousand euros per work was quickly offered in New York, and a run on his work already began.

Yet, it's impossible to obtain papers if you happen to stumble upon a Van Gogh, as happened to me, after which I even consciously began searching for more works.

There's even a story about a shop in Eindhoven that sold art supplies to Vincent – and regularly exchanged works for all sorts of items, probably painting materials as well – where four Van Goghs were indeed found in the attic.

One plus one equals two, you might say. This, too, wasn't taken seriously by the Van Gogh Museum and was barely investigated. These people, too, spent years obtaining the necessary documentation; without it, you can't sell them. The Van Gogh Museum in Amsterdam must have approved it; that's how it works, although it's not bound by any law or regulation. It's an unwritten rule that everyone adheres to, whether the investigation is serious or not; that's how it works. A bag of money can work in your favor; research is expensive.

But even so, my trust was gone.

I couldn't take it seriously anymore and decided not to consult them or call on them anymore. By then, the chips were down; you literally couldn't go anywhere, even though you couldn't anyway. Their research is taken very seriously worldwide, but in reality, it's often nothing more than a sham. There's usually no assessment of the work in reality.

If you have four paintings with the same discovery location, people seem unable to make a connection, or rather, they have little interest in it.

Many are familiar with the image of the famous painting with the bridge in France, or the sunflowers carefully placed on a table or in a specially made crate by museum staff wearing white gloves in a restoration studio.

They suggest very thorough research, while in reality, in many cases, nothing goes beyond an assessment based on a few photographs. That was the method, and now you can't get involved at all.

And this brings me to the second point about the conflict of interest: the management of the collection, which they want to keep private. Recognizing a work as a Van Gogh has major consequences. Firstly, for the owner of the work, who can become an instant millionaire, on paper. Secondly, the recognition adds a work to the globally renowned and recognized collection of works by Vincent van Gogh. Experts know exactly what he created, and hundreds of millions of books about his work have been sold. The moment a museum recognizes a work, it's added to the collection. You'd expect them to proceed cautiously; reliability is paramount, especially in this case. Nothing could be further from the truth, however. Works have been recognized that even laypeople claim weren't painted by Van Gogh. There appears to be a degree of subjectivity, which is utterly reprehensible in a case like this. This involves government funds that only a very select group, still controlled by the Van Gogh family, appears to benefit.

The Van Gogh Church

Some time ago, I came across another work by Vincent van Gogh through an online search, two even, or at least that's what was more or less suggested. I decided to make an offer and eventually reached an agreement with both parties, meaning for both works.

Due to the damage to my car—mainly after my husband's death, but also during his illness—I still don't have a car and have decided to do without it for a while, which I'm not happy about, but circumstances have forced me to do. As a result, I can't easily pick up a painting somewhere, as I have in the past. It requires creativity and adaptability, which is sometimes downright difficult, as in this case, because neither seller was very inclined to ship the works.

In the end, we agreed that personal delivery was an option. How coincidental, they both lived in Nuenen or nearby, not far from me, but they probably had nothing to do with each other. After some time, they arrived separately, within the same week, to bring the work to me, with a few days between them. One came from Geldrop, the other from Nuenen itself—the two villages are very close together. The man from Geldrop had to visit someone in Nuenen before coming to me. In this case, it was a painting of the Van Gogh Church.

The other, the one from Nuenen, arrived first. I was quite nervous, and I hadn't often had a private individual bring something to my home since becoming a widow. The transaction itself went smoothly, however, except that this was absolutely not a painting by Vincent van Gogh, I initially thought. Which was ultimately my goal: to find another Van Gogh.

The point is that commissioning official research into authenticity at the Van Gogh Museum has become nearly impossible. It was already very difficult, and it has become even more so in the past year. Disillusioned, many people offer their works online at low prices out of desperation. In the past, the Van Gogh Museum received an average of one work per day, for the size of the collection, and moreover, everything was usually rejected. It's difficult to judge that yourself; you need an expert, which is what I've become after all these years of research. I pick out the works effortlessly, although I sometimes make a bad purchase, about ten percent of the time.

At first glance, this seemed like a bad purchase. From a distance, I could already see that this work couldn't possibly have been painted by Vincent van Gogh; it looked very amateurish, which hadn't been very clear in the photo.

I concluded, and I still think, that Anton Kerssemakers might have been the artist. I immediately lost interest in the work. My collection now consists only of original works; even lithographs and etchings are no longer part of the main collection, which focuses on two artists: Barton and Van Gogh. I really didn't need this man's hideous work, even though he meant well and I was so glad to have seen it. The canvas was very old, yet in a very distinctive, oblong format often used by Van Gogh. Later, I started to doubt it again; it probably came from Van Gogh's studio, Vincent's Atelier, as he sometimes called it. I suggested he take it back with him and paid for his travel expenses.

Knowing it might have been painted by Anton Kerssemakers had made him very happy; he didn't mind taking it back with him.

Number two, the same week, was even more exciting after what had happened the first time, but I had more success with the second work.

A beautiful painting, in my opinion more beautiful than The Potato Eaters and Poplar Avenue near Nuenen combined, namely an early work by Vincent van Gogh of the Van Gogh Church.

How beautiful! I still can't express how impressive it is, so subduedly painted, in muted colors, and yet so colorful thanks to the many nuances.

Typical Van Gogh, it couldn't be otherwise. Very old, the varnish has yellowed.

It's painted exactly as Vincent intended, using neutral tones within a very broad color palette, which, despite the use of many colors, still creates harmony. This may not be immediately apparent here, but it becomes increasingly clear in later works. Although his much later works are characterized by strong contrast, they still display that very broad color palette.

The work has roughly the same perspective as the much more famous Van Gogh church, which must be from a (slightly) later date. There is some confusion in the letters here as well. Efforts have always been made to determine which work it refers to through the letters. However, not everything is described. There are periods when the correspondence between Vincent and Theo was very low, or when there was hardly any contact at all, at least not by letter.

Personally, I think the painting I received was one of his first true oil paintings.

It is a completely unknown work; if you look closely at it, you can see the master's hand in the texture of the way the paint is applied to the canvas.

I was actually quite shocked to have received such a beautiful work. I immediately recognized it as a remarkable work. I paid the man who had come up the garden path. He left happily, and I was euphoric for a few days. I could almost jump for joy; this was a bull's-eye and so perfect.

It's an old painting; the varnish has been eroded by the ravages of time and could be removed. I'd rather not do that myself. I've had frames replaced here and there, or even replaced them myself, but I usually don't do much more than that.

Even the frame of this work is perfect. The corners often come loose over time, but this piece is still very well framed. Of course, the frame is light in color.

I noticed something important on the back of the work, although it could be further investigated.

Which suddenly made a "bad buy" I once made very useful: a reproduction of Sunflowers, produced by the Van Gogh Museum? A beautiful reproduction made and framed as if it were a real painting.

Because Van Gogh painted several Sunflowers, I bought it based on a photographic assessment, a method I've become accustomed to, which isn't always easy, but without a car, it's currently the only option. When I received it on the spot, I immediately realized it was a bad purchase.

Now, this work suddenly came in very handy. The Van Gogh Museum had even recreated the back of this reproduction of one of the Sunflowers exactly, as if it were an original.

I immediately recognized the way Van Gogh assembled the rope for the hanging system because I'd encountered it before, in one or more of Van Gogh's works in my collection. He sometimes made a loop in the rope, thinking he could hang the painting neatly. This may have been one reason his works didn't sell. You can never get a work straight on the wall that way; it will always hang crooked, and it's crucial in an exhibition that everything hangs straight next to and above each other. Later, Van Gogh or the framers to whom works were brought also used iron wire, without a loop, and that brings you much closer.

The Van Gogh church I entered also had the rope tied at the back in the same way, quite remarkable.

In the landscape around Gemert, you still see many elements that, through the paintings, recall the time of Vincent van Gogh's life, such as old farmhouses, watermills, but also windmills, bridges, pollard willows—too many to mention, really.

The Van Gogh Museum doesn't always benefit directly from yet another new discovery, let alone the time and budget to conduct thorough research, although they are recognized worldwide for this.

This isn't bound by any rules; it's rather an unwritten rule that the Van Gogh Museum is the appropriate institution for this. This has developed over time and become standard procedure.

While there is some movement in this regard, art world professionals have been complaining about it for decades, and in that respect, I'm not alone.

Café Terrace at Night

Vincent van Gogh created multiple versions of certain works, such as five Sunflowers, four Little Bridges at Langlois, two Poplar Avenue at Nuenen, and even two versions of Café Terrace at Night, also known as Terrasse du café le soir, Place du Forum, Arles.

Let me explain:

Ton de Brouwer, a respected Van Gogh expert from Nuenen and the founder of the museum there, describes in his book "Van Gogh and Nuenen" how Vincent often created multiple versions of a single painting, sometimes assisted by his friend Anton Kerssemakers.

This happened for various reasons, depending on the painting, the time period, and developments in Vincent's life. For example, there are two known versions of Autumn Landscape; he painted the Bridge at Langlois four times, and so on.

Luc Van Omme also writes about this in his book "The Suitcase of Caracas." I am the rightful owner of one of the two works in question here, Café Terrace at Night, one of the most beautiful works Van Gogh ever painted. The other is in the Kröller-Müller Museum in Otterlo.

Like "Avenue of Poplars near Nuenen," of which I also have a version, the original, this work also still has its original stretcher frame, which is a rarity in itself.

It has never been restored and therefore retains its original strength and color.

Although "Avenue of Poplars near Nuenen" remains completely intact despite its age, though a good cleaning wouldn't hurt and it is very fragile, this work, "Avenue of Café at Night," has some damage. There was a small hole in the canvas, barely visible from a distance and completely repairable by a skilled restorer; the restoration process is currently underway.

The stretcher frame is an eighteenth-century invention that became popular in the nineteenth century. Miter sawing must have quickly become a standard part of the stretcher frame's production; it dates back to around the same time that miter sawing began. Towards the end of the nineteenth century, when Vincent was working as a painter, mitered corner pieces were used. Vincent's brother Theo, an art dealer with Goupil & Co., was active in the top echelons of the art world at the time. He provided Vincent's painting materials and the funding for them. It wouldn't be surprising if Vincent used the best and most modern materials of the time. Geographically, Paris, where Theo lived, also represented the pinnacle of the art world at the time.

The first edition of the letters Vincent sent to his brother Theo dates from the early twentieth century.

Vincent's sister-in-law, Jo van Gogh-Bongers, preserved many of the letters.

Unlike the letters Theo sent to Vincent, which were usually torn up by the recipient immediately upon receipt, Vincent's letters to Theo have been preserved.

So, half of the correspondence still exists, while the other half was often burned by the recipient, Vincent; these were usually letters containing money.

Jo van Gogh-Bongers, who became a widow shortly after her marriage to Theo because Theo also died about six months after Vincent's death, had saved all of Vincent's letters.

She spent years organizing them, typing them all up, and then publishing them.

Much of what is known about Vincent van Gogh's life is based on the letters, although it should be noted that Jo van Gogh-Bongers deliberately omitted certain letters; these may have been rediscovered later.

She did not include letters that were too personal, problematic, or privacy-sensitive in this edition, she writes. The missing letters were also omitted from later editions of Vincent's letters. They constitute a chapter in themselves, partly because it wasn't that long ago that someone found a collection of letters in an old trunk, once part of a shipload from an old South American sailing ship that looked suspiciously like these missing letters.

This partly explains why little is known about the friendship between Vincent, the Van Gogh family, and Pieter Kruijsen.

The Van Gogh expert is Professor Blanc from Switzerland, who has recognized works in my possession. The Van Gogh Museum hasn't done any further research, only a cursory look at a few photographs of some of the works.

I know someone else in my neighborhood, near Nuenen, who has ten of them. They're stored in a locked attic. They were once exchanged for goods, namely garden furniture, with Mrs. Van Gogh in his family.

The Pineal Gland

G emert, where I live, was a Catholic farming village, also a principality, but above all, very Catholic. As you may know, Vincent's father, the pastor, forbade him from contact with farmers.

At one point, a story emerged that in the past, various high-ranking figures had indulged in extravagant scenes, mysterious Germanic rituals, orgies, and even the drinking of children's blood—a shocking story. It was suggested that there might be a connection to the exchange of Van Gogh paintings because they were so valuable. It's possible; in Boekel, where Prince Hendrik sometimes visited in those days, I found several works. We're talking about the early twentieth century. As I sit here writing this, not far from Boekel, it suddenly starts storming and thundering here—perhaps a sign. Let me quickly move on to something else, as it's a sensitive subject anyway. I would like to offer some explanation here about the pineal gland, which people thought could be stimulated by drinking children's blood, which is apparently highly addictive. It's also extremely shocking that this could happen and possibly still happens; there's a lot of evidence for it.

The third eye, as human intuition is also called, is usually most highly developed in children. As people get older, the pineal gland, another word for the pineal gland, can become calcified. This is grist to the mill of the rulers of the Western world; they don't want people to develop any kind of giftedness or sensitivity; keeping people ignorant is their position. This could be a reason for fluoride in drinking water; it has a direct effect on the pineal gland by causing its reduced function. Fluoride, in particular, causes a layer to form over it, the ultimate process of which is calcification. Fluoride has even been added to some spring waters, which brings us to the next question: whether drinking liters of water a day benefits your health or not. The pH of some spring waters is around 6, while it should be above 7, and a pH of literally six can cause cancer and be fatal. Something to think about: not everything you hear on TV is true, nor is what you read in the newspapers. Many people have reached a certain level of awareness, but it hasn't yet dawned on every corner of the world that governments can be corrupt, even though a four-year-old could figure it out.

Blue

Red has become blue and blue is red.

Nothing is what it seems. Political correction is a form of lying, expressing an opinion that isn't really yours, isn't the truth, but is generally well-received, allowing you to show that you're very sociable, while the reality can be quite different. It's a way of putting yourself on a stage, which narcissists often crave, so they can show everyone how good they are to others. They don't realize that shouldering the world's suffering also has a huge downside: countries become ungovernable, and the possibility of revolution arises. Not everyone is happy with a leader's supposedly sociable sentiments. People who have dedicated their lives wholeheartedly to their country see all their efforts annihilated. We had to do it together to give our children a chance. The reality is that we did it together, only to squander it. Children were deprived of opportunities, and the accumulated capital went to a war that has nothing to do with anything but lust. And to anyone in the world who even wanted to join, the borders were wide open. There was no help for your immediate loved ones; I experienced it firsthand. "Just go to the authorities," was the answer. As if they could solve everything. No, everyone was your loved one except the people who truly mattered in someone's life; they had to figure it out for themselves. I literally experienced it, and I'm not even exaggerating; it's too awful for words.

People wrongly blamed me for a lot. I had a serious brain injury and a broken back, while Richard was dying and no one else wanted to care for him, even after repeated requests. Sometimes I literally collapsed.

Almost thirty years ago, I had pulled him out of a very deep pit and given him a new life. The person who threatened me when we were planning to marry Richard was ultimately the one who took his life.

The trigger for it was on his birthday, shortly before my wedding. It was the moment he received a very strange book as a gift, which threatened me indirectly, or directly, depending on how you look at it. The book was about an artist who was getting married; just before the wedding, his future wife was horribly murdered.

I was getting married six months later. Richard was an artist; you'd be practically blind not to see the similarities, they said. Hard to believe, and it was all about money.

When I met Richard, he had hardly any possessions; we'd built them up together. Now that he was doing better, his ex-wife wanted him back, completely ignoring me and the new partner she already had before she left Richard. She kept a close eye on us through the children.

Jealousy in the art world is also a terrible thing. It started when I was just getting together with Richard. Nothing was sold at the exhibition in the castle's Donjon at the time, but an immense diptych with a key was destroyed. It's all too sad to put into words, and what happened here is completely disproportionate.

Yet we must always continue to trust God, no matter what. That may sound cynical, but it's not meant that way. God teaches us specifically not to cling to things, that our neighbor is far more important.

The Bible offers many guidelines, although it should be noted that besides truths, there are often also different interpretations possible. The Bible speaks relatively little about women; we must make that distinction; much is written in the "he" (pronounced "he"). What kind of

We must make distinctions; much is written in the "he" (he) form. However, what applies to a man doesn't necessarily apply to a woman, although this is a generalization. Much is meant for people in general, both men and women.

Men and women are very different from each other. The idea that someone could change their gender is utter nonsense and merely a way to make a lot of money. The fault lies with society. Not every woman likes Botox or always wearing high heels.

Accept people for who they are, without immediately judging them. Men have both feminine and masculine qualities and vice versa. There's no reason to immediately call in a surgeon.

That they scout children from the age of eight for this reason in the Netherlands is overstating it; it's really all about money. Wake up. Government money often plays a role as well. That's not okay. By the mid-twenties, the growth into adulthood is, on average, complete for people. Some people, however, never grow up and remain stuck in childhood, with all the consequences that entails. Give people the opportunity to develop normally. Sexuality is something you have to learn; it doesn't just happen naturally. The same applies to developing your intuition, self-esteem, and independence. Almost everything in life has to be learned, which is why a good upbringing is so important.

Six months ago, my foster mother also passed away.

The division of the inheritance was anything but fair. My foster father and half-sister didn't treat her well. They didn't want me to care for her, leaving me powerless. She went through hell, a hardship and great sorrow for me.

Whenever I visited her, I was often kicked out the door by the aforementioned couple, or one of them. My foster mother was left in the lurch. She never had the strength to change anything, and now she doesn't have it at all.

Behind the scenes, I've made numerous attempts to find good help for her. What's making things difficult for me is yet another inheritance issue whose settlement isn't being handled fairly, although you could say that something meant for you always ends up with you.

The loss of Richard and the way everyone abandoned me are still deeply saddening to me; words simply can't describe what I went through during that period.

What sometimes keeps me awake at night is injustice, the inhumane way people have been treated, myself included, putting it mildly. People who get away with the most horrific crimes because authorities look the other way. I can't go anywhere without a car, and public transport is no longer an option after receiving very serious threats. I have plenty to do, that's not the problem. Not being able to make appointments is extremely difficult, however. My security guards usually know where I am. The problem is that criminals are often aware of this as well, meaning I can almost only leave the house unexpectedly. I cared for Richard all alone for eight years when he was ill. Although the GP sent some caregivers remotely, they ultimately didn't do much. Due to a lack of medical help, he sank further and further into a psychosis. Time and again, I went to get help for him.

I expected more integrity from my foster sister - for a long time she was the manager of a very large healthcare institution - although this also fit seamlessly into the list of things she'd already dropped in my direction, and not just dropped, how false. I didn't recognize anything in her anymore of the cheerful, sweet girl she used to be. In turn, she was completely destroyed by her in-laws. Fortunately, that didn't happen to me. My in-laws were so kind and sweet that my husband's ex kept visiting my mother-in-law in the United States, even crawling into bed with her, even with her new husband, and still calling her "mother." Looking for, or perhaps searching, looking for, money. Everyone says you can't rely on your in-laws for anything. I was grateful to Mom and owe her many good things, especially Bible study and the strong faith she instilled in me. RIP Mary Lee Barton. She lived to a very old age, almost a hundred, and I still miss her.

I asked my GP for help, and each time, my request was ignored. Only after seven years did the GP personally come to investigate, probably after being pointed out his mistakes.

Day in, day out, I was stuck with a terminally ill man for years, completely paralyzed. He wasn't taken seriously, even though, medically speaking, psychosis is about the worst thing that can happen to a person, a kind of life-or-death situation.

My family, some of whom worked in healthcare, did nothing. They all looked the other way. I had suffered quite a few blows, both literally and figuratively, because of the situation, and there was hardly any help. My family just yelled from a distance, called authorities behind my back, and blamed me. It was pointless, but it had a huge impact, which was officially acknowledged afterward. You could say they obstructed help, and that's an understatement.

Things got worse and worse, and to make matters worse, they even vandalized my car, which Richard and I had saved up for so long; it was our hobby. How dare you, I thought to myself, I really needed that car, if only because of Richard's illness, for example, to transport his wheelchair and all sorts of things.

The windshield, once like new, was completely smeared with dog poop and sand, it had become covered in scratches and dents. I had to take it in for repairs, which I didn't even have time for. Richard was paralyzed and completely reliant on me for help. My family did nothing to help and was more likely to obstruct than to do anything good. It's also clear who was behind the vandalism of my car. Scratches were frequently made on my car. Every morning I had to check if some scoundrel had messed with it again. And I kept wondering why.

After Richard's death, it got even worse, as if I didn't have enough to worry about. They weren't just targeting my car but also his grave, vandalism happening again and again. I was hit from behind, and I eventually got rid of that car after repairs.

I found the vandalism at the grave almost worse, if not worse. Every time I went there, something happened: a temporary monument had been violently destroyed, and it didn't stop there. It was clear to me who the perpetrator was, and they continued to annoy me for years, standing at my window at night, doing the craziest things, the Romanian mafia chasing me. What happened in the vegetable garden is also directly related; the same perpetrator was behind all this. Someone in my family was severely abused throughout her childhood, starting when I was four years old. She blames me for it, and that's unfair. The real perpetrator never wanted to make things right, even unfairly, because I've been a victim of this my whole life. It's an unstoppable emotional rollercoaster, a dangerous figure from whom I've distanced myself forever. It was never my fault, but it was a fate I've had to bear for decades. I'm trying to put it behind me, including my contact with them. They think they have authority over you because they're family, which of course makes no sense, and they're only half family. They're brainless people who lash out and cause trouble everywhere. Staying away is best.

When my husband died, he told me a lot in the last days of his life that I didn't know, especially about my family. He'd known them much longer than I'd known him, and I didn't even know that.

So it turns out my father was my foster father. Both parents were probably foster parents. I have no reason to doubt Richard's stories, and it got much worse. They even asked him to kill me. I see my foster father as the perpetrator. My foster mother had a good character, but she was also severely abused by him.

Abuse runs like a thread through my foster father's life. He was guilty of it many times, and I suspect him of criminal offenses. One of those is that, for no apparent reason, towards the end of my studies, he wrestled me to the ground, stomped on my back, and kicked me in the head. Just like that, out of nowhere. I was so stunned that I couldn't react to defend myself. It had serious consequences for my life; something snapped. After everything I'd been through with him, probably literally, including brain damage, and the damage to my left ear, which he kicked, has always bothered me. He's a difficult man, impossible to reason with, and he completely turned my half-sister against me, which is even worse.

All of this was probably due to an inheritance from my biological father, of which I never received a penny. I've found a lot of evidence for this, including that he must have left a lot, and that it was kept from me.

That's probably why my foster father wanted to kill me. That makes you sick, after all. He's been abusing me since I was a child. I never really understood it until Richard told me a lot about it a few years ago.

A third matter concerns compensation for someone's use of an antipsychotic medication. Due to lies from family, I was misdiagnosed and wrongly forced to take that very medication for years. They went so far, my half-sister and my foster father, as to commission a book about me, full of lies and deceit, based on stolen medical records and a diary my foster father kept about me, who was already quite ill in itself. This book is called "Everything is Carmen," and it is extremely serious libel and slander. I tried to have it withdrawn from circulation, but I failed. It's even available for loan from the public library; half of Gemert has read it. It's truly appalling how, out of jealousy and for money, they even threw my medical records out into the open, and it's all just gossip and slander.

My life was destroyed by them. I couldn't make a career. Everything I tried to build with Richard was destroyed just as brutally by them. It's beyond words.

They commissioned the book, authored by Alma Mathijssen, possibly because of that compensation. Someone from Canada received a whopping eight billion from a pharmaceutical company. Probably a cousin of mine who lives in Canada. He called me around the time it happened to tell me I had a brother, but he didn't elaborate. I've since come to understand; his behavior revealed he suddenly had considerable money. I wasn't informed of this either, and I haven't seen a cent of it.

They must have been very pathetic and complained about the impact of the drug, which they felt, was a factor in their behavior.

I even had trouble with my family. That was ridiculous; I never had any contact with him. That company was probably put under immense pressure; it's disproportionate compensation for people who behave disproportionately and with whom I don't want to have much to do.

I was harassed a lot by my half-sister, and neighbors also caused Richard and me an excessive amount of trouble. We experienced the craziest things. I didn't really understand the reasons for it all at the time, but in hindsight, I understand. There were robberies, several burglaries, and things stolen. One evening, a neighbor—fortunately, he no longer lives next door—even came to hack at our front door.

This is just a small sample of the many criminal acts committed against me. Richard couldn't survive this. Neither could my foster mother; she stood by me and was also severely abused by them. This also happened for political reasons. As family members, you should be able to have healthy discussions. I was always silenced, kicked out the door, something I can no longer tolerate. They even tried to bribe the police. In the end, I was proven right; the truth always wins.

To stop them, I started writing this book.

My foster parents were married in community of property and never told me I wasn't their biological child, something I understand in hindsight. At the time, I didn't understand why, as the eldest child, I was completely ignored when it came to accessing their estate. If they had informed me sooner, I might have been able to claim compensation from the church, but now I'm literally stuck between the stool and the ashes. My foster mother didn't want this and saw me as her daughter. Not only that, but we were friends.

They had a will drawn up together. I was kept out of everything and learned nothing. They told me nothing, even though I have the same rights as my two sisters; on paper, they are my biological parents. I can assume things went differently, but that hasn't been proven anywhere. I did consider having a DNA test done with Maxima, Queen of the Netherlands, because she had asked me to. At that time, the Government Information Service (RVO) didn't want it to be known that I might be her sister, so I'm convinced there's no need to start such a test. The situation has changed over the years, but there still hasn't been a test.

Richard could claim they weren't my biological parents, but they never told me directly. It was a suspicion; on paper, they were still just my parents.

So, fraud was committed during the will's preparation. My foster mother didn't want me to receive just the child's share; she disagreed. It's inevitable that my foster father, foster sister, and her partner forged my foster mother's signature; a third party investigated. My half-sister also confirmed some things by phone. My foster sister had gone to the notary with my foster father a few years ago, without my mother being present, which in itself was very strange and indicative of the situation. My mother wasn't ill at the time, although that changed quite quickly. Changes were made, meaning I only get the child's share, which is just too awful to put into words. The child's share was lost after the

There's nothing about debt settlement, it's a sixth. How devious they all are! They must have calculated it down to the last cent, that's how far I know them.

They even attempted to take my life for that very reason, and they are also at least partly to blame for the deaths of my mother and my husband. It's all too pathetic to put into words, crimes against life for a small sum of money. What they did was completely inhumane.

I finally asked the notary in question for a copy of the will. My foster father had promised a copy, but I received one with a lot of text missing, probably poorly copied on purpose because he wasn't willing to provide a proper copy. I was kicked out for the umpteenth time.

I also asked my foster sister for a copy; she was appointed executor, according to the supplementary will I recently read. She literally said: "This is not my will, and it's not up to me to provide you with those papers." Almost laughable, first of all, she unlawfully arranged for the addition to the will, together with my foster father, by forging a signature because my foster mother disagreed. Her words should be turned around; it seems like her will, and figuratively speaking, it was, almost literally. Only, her signature wasn't on it because my mother should have signed it. So that probably didn't happen; it might also have been my foster sister's signature, though I'm more likely to believe my father ultimately forged the signature. The addition is full of names I don't recognize, legacies, and who knows what else, all in favor of my foster sister, who arranged this addition. If this is carried out, there will be nothing left for me, which also applies to my half-sister, even though she's already had her share. That's also very unfair. My mother never wanted anything other than for everything to be divided fairly among the children. After they had stripped me of everything, as the eldest child, I was also stripped of my role as executor of the will. Without any consultation, everything was passed on to my foster sister, who is five years younger.

I consider both my foster sister and my foster father incompetent. Secondly, it's so ridiculous because it's practically her will, which is what makes it so ludicrous. The document, which I had the right to inspect and which I finally received from the notary a few weeks later for ninety euros, is filled with the names of her children and bequests to them, making me sick. All my life, I've been made all sorts of promises, and she, the youngest daughter, simply brushed them aside as if they were nothing, even though she already has so much money, unlike her sisters. I had to pay ninety euros to get a copy of the will from the notary. I have the right to inspect it. It's all beyond words, especially considering how my mother has been treated by my father in recent years. She didn't agree with this.

Kidnapped

It wasn't the first time. During that period, I took a taxi to escape from home again. According to Richard, I no longer lived in our shared house, and he made that very clear to me. Time and again, I had to flee because of the aggression he had developed due to his fear of death. The lack of support for him while he had fallen into a very serious psychosis was beyond my control, and no one was willing to help. Whenever I fled again and tried to reach him by phone, I was invariably told: "You don't live here anymore!" If he even answered.

A taxi driver who was supposed to take me to a hotel, something I had just managed to arrange, drove off in the middle of the night to a dark forest. I had to struggle to get home safe and sound. His intentions were anything but good. First of all, there were plenty of hotels much closer to home; I didn't need to go to Rosmalen for that, and in retrospect, I wonder if the enormous hotel he initially mentioned was even there. We never arrived anyway and ended up in the middle of a dark forest where he ordered me out. I knew in my gut that this was a serious matter. The friend he'd called on the way over the loudspeakers wasn't going to help, that much was clear, even though he pretended to be the hotel receptionist, or at least that's the lie the driver called him.

At the beginning of the ride, he'd tricked me into withdrawing a lot of money, because I'd have to stay at the hotel for a while. I'd sat in the back; it was as if he'd been expecting my call; he came up with a ready-made story about a similar situation. I held on tightly to my walking stick—which I used at the time, due to the brain injury I sustained from all the hectic activity; I couldn't walk properly at that point. Even when he ordered me out, I took charge of this miserable situation: "And now you're going to take me back to Gemert immediately!"

He thought for a moment and ordered me back in the car. I took a seat in the back again, still clutching my walking stick.

We wandered around for a while.

Finally, he took the route back along the canal.

I still didn't feel safe at all.

There was no traffic on the road at that hour of night, completely silent.

I felt utterly exhausted and expected to have to get out again at any moment. Fortunately, that moment didn't happen, even though it was an eternity of a half hour along the canal.

Finally, we ended up on the way back to the village.

I still had the feeling he could take a different route at any moment; we weren't there yet.

He had been silent the whole way, whereas he had been so talkative on the way there.

I offered to pay him upfront and, on top of the enormous amount, gave him a huge tip to get me out of this situation.

It worked; at least I hadn't withdrawn the money for nothing.

He took me back anyway and at the end of the ride told me never to take a taxi again.

I have good reason to believe that Tanja Groen also survived her even more perilous adventure, although I cannot comment further on this at this time. The Dutch authorities are aware of this, and she is being deliberately kept out of the public eye.

Due to the seriousness of the case, her health has become fragile, she lives in anonymity, and is no longer the Tanja Groen we know from the photo. It goes without saying that this case will be pursued further.

God is wisdom

His Word, the Bible, is all about wisdom; love for your neighbor; justice; only good qualities. It is not human wisdom, but divine wisdom, that will take you far.

The aromas of integrity and purity are fresh. A person's character is reflected in their surroundings. The Bible can help you with this. Through the Word of God, you learn how to treat your fellow man; how to be successful in life. Especially that you must forgive; otherwise, no blessings are possible. Christ died on the cross for the forgiveness of our sins.

Purity, integrity, and truth are divine values that can take you far in life. Man is a spiritual being; the body is sensory. Purity and wisdom permeate everything. Living in His grace brings you freedom. I don't mean the freedom of a joint and a beer at a beach bar; that is, in reality, bondage. Freedom from sin brings you health and freedom! The Bible tells us to stay away from evil people. The book of Proverbs, in particular, contains many life lessons that can give you direction. Just read it. Bible study is important. It helps us live more wisely. Making decisions based on emotions is unwise. Thinking three times before you say or do something will help you move forward. Anyone who thinks evil people don't exist should think twice. They can have a negative impact on someone's life. And you don't just change people overnight. Be on your guard. Silence is often best. There's already enough judgment in this world. Yet, I would like to share my opinion here about a world without borders, a world dominated by lust, by the hunger for money and power. It brings you nothing. A world without borders brings misery and is so impersonal that normal governance is impossible. The world is like a rudderless ship ruled by computers, a Titanic. Everyone needs borders. Borderlessness brings much unhappiness. Freedom exists because of the presence of borders. There is no freedom without constraints. Unless you think a joint or whatever gives you freedom, it's a false sense of freedom; the "pleasure" only lasts for a moment. What remains is a craving for addiction. Addictions are the opposite of freedom, so we need boundaries. Not everything is good for you; quite the opposite!

Your body is the palace you live in. The path to heaven is narrow, and it's difficult to stay on it, yet there is no other way. The gray, wide highway leads nowhere. The only path is to God's love. Or call it the laws of nature, that's also possible. Everything we need is already here: plants, animals, water, and so on. It all multiplies. Just as everyone receives God's grace, you don't have to do anything for it. He sent His Son to earth for forgiveness.

By having faith and doing good things, you will receive them. God represents everything that is good, such as honesty, integrity, love, you name it. Compassion is important. His word is recorded in the Bible, so study is essential to live in His spirit. We can live without religion, but not without Bible study. You must understand what it's about: how we can sustain the earth.

You are a spirit, living in a body, and having a soul. If you live healthily, according to the spirit of the Word, it has a healing effect on both body and soul. Take care of yourself, just as you would take care of yourself.

If you love something, you should especially be on your body. Plants cared for with love will thrive. This also applies to humans; you only have one body and one life, you have to make do with it. While it's sometimes important to dare to take a gamble, gambling with your life is very unwise. Eternal life exists and is preferable to hell; I can tell you all about that. Choose the good!

We give houses to complete strangers, and our neighbors are pushed off the list. The current problems largely stem from ruthless human traffickers.

I want to talk about something else for a moment. I might get angry and, like so many others, I don't want to be led by emotions.

Even if my path leads through dark chasms. A line from a psalm I recently memorized.

In recent weeks, I've been reading a lot about crime in the 1930s. There are still entire reports of confessions and investigations from that period. A convicted offender explained it this way: "As young people, we had no entertainment, so we just went looking for it in the pub, didn't save up for a day out." It reminds me of a situation where a municipality chooses to build a costly golf club over a decent outdoor pool that many more people could enjoy.

Ultimately, you often have to do it yourself. The welfare state has proven to be a utopia, perhaps for the best. It's every man for himself and God for us all. After all, He sees everything and can count the hairs on your head. The reckoning comes at the gates of heaven. God is love and wisdom. The Bible speaks of charity, but it doesn't mean you should endanger yourself by helping someone else. Your body is the palace you live in.

By wanting to help others, we sometimes endanger ourselves. Often just to be able to express how much compassion we have, for example, with refugees. Yet, fleeing doesn't always help, in fact, never does. You always carry your problems with you. For example, there have been problems in Syria since the 60s. We can't solve this by bringing them all here; it disrupts society, which is becoming completely overloaded. Because it's not just Syrians; it's half of Africa, Eastern Europe, the Middle East. You're out of your mind if you think you can solve all this as a mini-city-state. Think of cities like New York and Paris; the problems there are currently incalculable. In New York alone, more than three hundred thousand people spend the night on the streets as homeless. A small-scale approach offers far more solutions; then it all remains somewhat manageable, and the human character is preserved.

The images are so profound that they're hard to shake. Europe is slowly transforming from a relatively stable continent with many cultural facets—think of all those different countries and their beautiful cities—into a macabre, ghostly landscape. Lying in the grass dreaming of a bright future is no longer possible; it's being mown down from under your feet.

Man is a ghost. Violence, even verbal violence, can be a terrible thing. It reminds me of a caregiver who told a patient week after week: "You have to accept that you can't do anything." That patient was me once, a recently graduated Exercise Scientist at the time. Opposite me was another recently graduated scientist, in psychology. For six years, I heard it every week; she didn't want to know anything about my past, what a slap in the face. And it became

Worse still, based on gossip and slander from family, she managed to label me with one of the most horrific medical diagnoses imaginable, which, incidentally, no medical specialist agreed with, and they had actually studied for it.

That's pure mental abuse, not counseling. You never know who you're dealing with. Don't trust just anyone.

I'm going to continue studying the Bible. It's wonderful to constantly learn new things about acting justly and how to attract good things. It's fascinating how much positive energy that can generate. Just by speaking positive words. It's not necessary for everyone to focus on the current problems in Europe. Leave it to the people who are designated for it. Furthermore, make sure you have a good day, every day. Ultimately, that's what matters. Heaven on earth really does exist.

Regularly, though only very sporadically at the moment, I sometimes go to pray in a chapel in a nursing home. I once had an apparition of God there. He was sitting in a chair across from me, talking to me. The door to that chapel is often open. When I go in, I close it. It often happens that while I'm sitting there, the door is abruptly flung open. A domestic worker who thinks the door should be open, they don't look to see if anyone's there, the door swings open, and they walk on.

The other day, I put a Bible there. A room without books is a room without a soul. Often, one finds statues of Mary in prayer rooms. She was a remarkable woman, but the first commandment is: "You shall worship no other images." This means, according to Protestants, nothing other than God the Father, His Son, and the Holy Spirit. You can also see it more broadly: Mary also belongs to the entire curriculum of faith, to put it bluntly. The point is that worshipping Coca-Cola, Yab Yum, or whatever other heroes you might have in mind are different images, truly different images. One of my hobbies was Feng Shui. This is the theory of how a home's location and layout influence your happiness and health. For example, a sofa against a wall feels more comfortable than one in front of a window. Having your back to a door or window is equally unpleasant. Water should be in front of your house, not behind it; moreover, it should flow. The signs of the zodiac can also be used. Depending on your date of birth, a calculation can be made that determines the most favorable orientation for your front door.

For example, it's unfavorable if there's a T-junction in front of your house and a road runs directly towards you. Living near a cemetery is also considered unfavorable according to Feng Shui. I could go on, but this isn't the core of my argument.

The point is that there can be overlap; we can learn something from Hinduism and from Buddhists. However, it's important that we don't forget the suffering of Christ; He was the only son of God. In terms of content, the Bible is incomparable to any other book; everything pales in comparison. We can write books to supplement it, explain it, and offer perspectives. It disproportionates the Quran; to state that you must kill anyone who isn't your brother or sister makes it a criminal document. And if copyright had existed back then, it wouldn't have even been created.

Over the past few days, I've been studying the Bible a lot. God promised us, in the days of Noah, that he would never again completely cover the earth with water.

God created the earth in such a way that everything is already there. Every plant, every animal, every living organism has, in principle, the ability to reproduce.

In the days of Noah, people lived to be very old. Noah lived to be twelve hundred years old, and he had his first child when he was one hundred and twenty. Generation after generation, his descendants lived less and less long. What was striking was that they had children at increasingly younger ages.

I also see the Revelation of John differently. People keep coming up with stories about the world ending, but it's much more about the suffering that can affect someone personally. As soon as you become seriously ill, that's what can happen to you. That all the floodgates open, there's no stopping you, until Christ comes. He is the one who brings salvation. If one has always walked in God's ways, it doesn't have to come to this; then salvation is always much closer.

Sometimes I visit churches I've never been to before. One day, hidden beneath beautiful, large trees, I arrived at one of the most beautiful churches in the Netherlands. A church that draws people from all over. I see God there even before I'm even inside; the light plays beautifully through the trees.

I was amazed when I first saw the pastor. She was dressed in an enormous robe. It seemed so surreal from the pulpit, which was about a meter higher.

The problem is I can't follow her well. I listen very attentively to men, but with women, I sometimes drift off, or I don't find it inspiring enough. I suddenly woke up when she started talking about bread and spiritual food. That Christ is not only the salt of the earth, but also the leaven in the bread. That if there's no leaven, you get a failure.

Silentium! Did I hear that right?

Isn't that basic group four? It's certainly not high politics, to put it that way. First of all, I find the word "misfire" inappropriate in a church, especially coming from a pastor. I was slightly shocked and wondered if it was really a church I'd entered that day and if I would even be allowed to share in the bread and wine they had prepared for a special occasion.

Yet, I think there's often a reason why churches are empty. A Protestant service is fantastic, wonderful to sing all those hymns, but what a shame they're only half-sung. There are Orthodox services that last for hours. It's a constant search for the right verse. Why don't they take the time on Sunday, the Lord's Day?

Quite a few people get sour looks when you mention Jesus. It's a shame; only through him can you come to God. By his blood we are saved, not because we do so much charity or work so hard. Only by believing in him do we receive God's grace. Strictly following the laws isn't essential in itself; God's grace is far greater. You sometimes see people who have no faith, except in themselves or matter, but not in a higher power, that they think they will be rewarded by the hopeless pursuit of rules. Of course,

Living according to God's laws is good, but I'm talking about something else here: sticking to rules at the expense of humanity.

The words God and Jesus bring to mind love, while fearing God is an equally important aspect of faith. God helps you in His moment; He gives you what He thinks you need.

Without faith, a happy life is impossible. He gives you the confidence to persevere and overcome in moments of weakness. Moreover, He grants peace. He is a living God and doesn't fit the outdated image that people often create; that is, what people have created of him.

Only through Bible study can you learn about God and divine wisdom.

A magnet has a magnetic field and therefore attracts or repels other magnets. The poles of the magnet are where the magnetic force is strongest. The north pole attracts a south pole and vice versa. Two north poles repel each other, and this also applies to south poles. The direction and strength of magnetic forces can be visualized using field lines. In relationships of any kind, similar forces can be unleashed, though there's not always an immediate explanation for this. In that respect, people are sometimes like magnets. In some cases, you can even actually feel a small electric shock upon contact, both positive and negative. It can sometimes be difficult to resist, especially when dealing with very powerful charges.

That's simply how God created the world. That He has the final say became clear in the time of Noah. Everyone knows the story of the ark. God chose Noah because He felt the rest of humanity had made a mess of things and weren't following His laws. You all know how it ended. It's difficult to fight the powerful forces of nature. It's easier to go with the flow and trust in God's goodness.

That we should fear God is the other side of the coin. The story of Noah clearly illustrates that He can punish harshly. Following the laws begins with gaining knowledge about them. It's not something that comes naturally; Bible study and the correct explanation are very important for this. The most beautiful passage in the Bible is found in the book of Wisdom in the deuterocanonical books:

22 Wisdom, the maker of all things, has instructed me. Her spirit is wise, holy, unique, versatile, refined, mobile, clear, pure, accessible, invulnerable, loving, shrewd, 23 irrepressible, benevolent, charitable, steadfast, immovable, untroubled, almighty, overseeing everything and penetrating all spirits, no matter how sharp, pure, or subtle. 24 Wisdom is more mobile than all that moves; she penetrates and permeates all things with her purity. 25 She is the breath of God's power, the pure radiance of the glory of the Almighty; no unclean thing can enter her. 26 In her shines the eternal light; in her the power of God is reflected flawlessly, and his goodness is pictured. 27 She is one, yet she can do all things; she is unchangeable, yet she renews all things. She passes on to every generation of godly people and makes them friends of God and prophets. 28 For God loves only those who share in wisdom. 29 In beauty she excels the sun, her place is above the stars. She is more excellent than the daylight, 30 for the night follows the day, but wisdom is never obscured by evil. (Wisdom 7:22-30)

God is wisdom. His Word, the Bible, is all about wisdom, love for your neighbor, justice, and so on. It is not human wisdom, but divine wisdom that will take you far.

A lover of silence once said, "I rarely talk long with people without suffering injury to my conscience." Another said, "It must be an uplifting word that is better than silence." A third said, "Noble is the word spoken at the right time." And a fourth added, "He who keeps his mouth shut does not slander or lie." Oh, how praiseworthy and pleasing is the word of the speaker that is not mixed with evil, vanity, deceit, or falsehood! Many people say many things, but not without the danger of the tongue inclined to evil. But there is much peace in those who keep their mouths shut, who stay in jail, and pray often.

Deepak Chopra once told a story about two goddesses: the goddess of money and the goddess of wisdom. If you pay too much attention to the goddess of money, she'll run away and want nothing to do with you. However, if you pay attention to the goddess of wisdom, the goddess of money will become jealous and come to you. Money will come to you if you show a good heart, for example, by helping others. You'll never be bored in that regard, because there's always someone you can help; the gratitude you often receive for that is better than any antidepressant.

On a completely different note, the number of transgender people in our country is increasing dramatically. Even children who haven't yet reached adulthood are already being registered at the VU University Medical Center. My goodness, that really gives food for thought; I'll leave my actual thoughts on this aside for now. It's a bit surreal. It's impossible to turn a man into a woman and vice versa. And children of that age haven't yet had the chance to properly develop their sexuality. It's also something that needs to be learned.

Sexuality within the confines of marriage can be an ultimate divine experience, at least if it's nourished by love.

It's a sensitive topic; it's rarely discussed in a positive way, even though it can be an experience that makes the stars fall from the sky. God didn't give us butterflies for nothing; they are the angels of the Holy Spirit who show us the way. However, it's important to build your house on a rock.

We should let go of the idea of the human psyche a bit, because it brings many problems. When you delve into someone's psyche, it immediately becomes complicated and unleashes things that are better left alone. It's better to use the word "spiritual." Humans are spirits. Everyone can interpret this in their own way. Living in the spirit of God is good, but there are plenty of people who place more value on material things, which can fill their spirits—the absolute opposite of God. Mammon is the Syriac word for the worship of money, which is devilish.

Therefore, humans are spirits and have souls, which consist of feelings, memories, experiences, and so on. The human soul can be positively influenced by one's spirit.

God represents the good, such as wisdom, love, and justice. Their positive influence is self-evident. Finally, humans live in a body that responds to the senses. However, according to biblical principles, one should not always give in to physical needs, also known as the flesh. It is important to apply God's spiritual wisdom in your life. This has a good influence on the soul, but also on the body. For example, not giving in to excessive drinking, overeating, and the like—that is, lust.

The Bible speaks of marriage because only then can the "use" of each other be prevented, which brings balance.

It is important not to confuse love and lust. Both terms can refer to sex, a significant way for most people to make life exciting and enjoyable, or bearable. While the former can be something very beautiful: love, the most divine thing there is; the latter is reprehensible: lust. The promiscuity of Western society is at odds with many Eastern beliefs, but it's also difficult to reconcile with Christianity. True Christians familiar with the Bible often know that it's written that a man shouldn't lie next to a man. It's also very humiliating for a woman, especially men who hate women. Dutch schools are eagerly teaching about anal sex. It's not only unclean, but also very dangerous, with risks including bowel perforation, stretched sphincters, and HIV infections. The risk of HIV is many times greater during anal sex, especially for the recipient—the term alone! It's the worst kind of torture and not intended as such. The sphincter stimulates the body to release waste; it has little to do with sex. It's a misconception to think so. How shocking it must be for young people to have their first experience with sexuality in this way—very frightening, of course. In that sense, there's a lot to be said about how other cultures approach virginity and sexuality.

Children used to learn to wash their hands in school after using the toilet. Now they learn about anal sex, how to kiss someone's anus, or rimming—it's truly beyond words. How terribly unclean, how can you even reconcile it? People think it's modern, but in reality, it's rather backward. You wouldn't put gold down a drain, would you?

People have come to consider it normal, but it's a source of misery. If you think about it a little more, you'd immediately conclude that it's rather illogical behavior.

After all, no one likes to play Russian roulette, even though many people do. It's as if they're switching off their brains. They're following their senses, their lust. That's why wisdom is so important. Use your head; you didn't get it for nothing! Lust is not good; it has little to do with love.

Disclaimer

While the information in this book has been compiled with great care, the author accepts no liability for any direct or indirect damage (of any kind) arising from or in any way related to its content. No rights can be derived from it.

The author accepts no responsibility for any organizations, companies, individuals, etc., referred to in this book and cannot be held liable for any events resulting from its content.

The Bible text in this publication is taken from The New Bible Translation, © Netherlands Bible Society 2004/2007.

Bio

*D*uring COVID-19 I was involved in politics as a volunteer and I'm also the owner of a huge private art collection, in fact I am a medical scientist specialized in human physical movement.

www.carmenbarton.com

www.ingramcontent.com/pod-product-compliance
Lightning Source LLC
Chambersburg PA
CBHW021638120626
46545CB00002B/598